Upper Columbia Basin Network Integrated Water Quality Annual Report 2011

Nez Perce National Historical Park (NEPE)

Natural Resource Technical Report NPS/UCBN/NRTR—2012/571

Eric Starkey

Aquatic Biologist
Upper Columbia Basin Network Inventory and Monitoring Program
105 E. 2nd St.
Suite #7
Moscow, ID 83843

April 2012

U.S. Department of the Interior
National Park Service
Natural Resource Stewardship and Science
Fort Collins, Colorado

The National Park Service, Natural Resource Stewardship and Science office in Fort Collins, Colorado publishes a range of reports that address natural resource topics of interest and applicability to a broad audience in the National Park Service and others in natural resource management, including scientists, conservation and environmental constituencies, and the public.

The Natural Resource Technical Report Series is used to disseminate results of scientific studies in the physical, biological, and social sciences for both the advancement of science and the achievement of the National Park Service mission. The series provides contributors with a forum for displaying comprehensive data that are often deleted from journals because of page limitations.

All manuscripts in the series receive the appropriate level of peer review to ensure that the information is scientifically credible, technically accurate, appropriately written for the intended audience, and designed and published in a professional manner. Data in this report were collected and analyzed using methods based on established, peer-reviewed protocols and were analyzed and interpreted within the guidelines of the protocols.

Views, statements, findings, conclusions, recommendations, and data in this report do not necessarily reflect views and policies of the National Park Service, U.S. Department of the Interior. Mention of trade names or commercial products does not constitute endorsement or recommendation for use by the U.S. Government.

This report is available from the Upper Columbia Basin Network (http://www.nature.nps.gov/im/units/ucbn/) and the Natural Resource Publications Management website (http://www.nature.nps.gov/publications/nrpm/).

Please cite this publication as:

NPS 429/113809, April 2012

Contents

Contents (continued)

Figures

Tables

Tables (continued)

Appendices

Executive Summary

The mission of the National Park Service is "to conserve unimpaired the natural and cultural resources and values of the national park system for the enjoyment of this and future generations" (NPS 1999). To uphold this goal, the Director of the NPS approved the Natural Resource Challenge to encourage national parks to focus on the preservation of the nation's natural heritage through science, natural resource inventories, and expanded resource monitoring (NPS 1999). Through the Challenge, 270 parks in the national park system were organized into 32 inventory and monitoring networks. The Upper Columbia Basin Network (UCBN) is comprised of 8 national park sites located in Idaho, Montana, Oregon, and Washington.

The UCBN has identified 14 priority park vital signs, indicators of ecosystem health, which represent a broad suite of ecological phenomena operating across multiple temporal and spatial scales. The intent of the network is to monitor a balanced and integrated "package" of vital signs that meets the needs of current park management, but will also be able to accommodate unanticipated environmental conditions in the future. Water quality is a particularly high priority vital sign for six of the nine UCBN parks. The UCBN contains more than 34 rivers, streams, ponds, and reservoirs. Unlike many National Parks that are large and often encompass entire watersheds, most UCBN parks and water bodies are small and embedded in large watersheds with diverse land use.

This annual report details the status of key indicators of water quality obtained from monitoring in Nez Perce National Historical Park (NEPE). Monitoring occurred in two units of NEPE, Spalding and Weippie Prairie. Lapwai Creek flows through the Spalding unit and Jim Ford Creek flows through the Weippe Prairie unit. Lapwai Creek was previously sampled by the UCBN in 2008 (see Starkey 2009), while 2011 is the first year of sampling Jim Ford Creek. Data from the 2011 field sampling effort was collected following methods detailed in the UCBN integrated water quality monitoring protocol (Starkey et al. 2008). The UCBN Integrated Water Quality Monitoring Protocol was formally peer-reviewed and approved for implementation in August 2009. This protocol can be found on the UCBN website at: http://science.nature.nps.gov/im/units/ucbn/reports/index.cfm#IWQ_Mon. Benthic macroinvertebrates were collected by the United States Forest Service- PACFISH/INFISH Biological Opinion (PIBO) according to their peer reviewed protocol during the UCBN's monitoring of stream channel characteristics and riparian condition in 2011. The UCBN's peer reviewed stream channel characteristics and riparian condition protocols can also be found on the UCBN's website listed above.

Water chemistry and macroinvertebrate results indicate that Jim Ford and Lapwai Creeks are in fair condition, with the primary concerns being elevated water temperatures, and pH levels above established thresholds. The status of water quality for Jim Ford and Lapwai Creeks relative to state regulatory thresholds is given in the summary tables on the following page. UCBN water quality monitoring is conducted on a 3 year rotating panel. As a result, conditions in both Jim Ford and Lapwai Creek will be re-evaluated in 2014.

Note that several of the appendices in this report are primarily intended for UCBN internal reference. In addition, some appendices serve as hard copies of quality assurance/quality control procedures performed during data processing.

Jim Ford Creek Water Chemistry Summary 2011

Measure	Current Condition (June-October, 2011)	State DEQ Thresholds[a]	% Exceedance[b]
Temperature (*MDMT, **MDAT)	* MDMT= 22.26 °C ** MDAT= 21.68 °C	*MDMT<22 °C **MDAT<19 °C	5 % 42%
Specific conductance (mean)	108.7 µS/cm	N/A	N/A
Dissolved oxygen (mean daily min)	6.6 mg/l	> 6.0 mg/l	1 %
pH (mean daily max)	7.36 pH Units	9.0 pH Units, Max	0%
pH (mean daily min)	7.12 pH Units	6.5 pH Units, Min	0%
Turbidity (mean daily max)	--[c]	< 50 NTU over background (instantaneous) < 25 for 10 consecutive days	Insufficient data
E. coli	33.5 MPN/100 ml	< 406 *E. coli*/100 ml	0%
Fecal Coliform	33 MPN/100 ml	<500 cfu/100 ml	0%

Lapwai Creek Water Chemistry Summary 2011

Measure	Current Condition (June-November, 2011)	State DEQ Thresholds[d]	% Exceedance[b]
Temperature (*MDMT, **MDAT)	* MDMT= 24.31 °C ** MDAT= 21.04 °C	*MDMT<22 °C **MDAT<19 °C	27% 17%
Specific conductance (mean)	273.19 µS/cm	N/A	N/A
Dissolved oxygen (mean daily min)	8.24 mg/L	> 6.0 mg/L	0%
pH (mean daily max)	9.0 pH Units	9.0 pH Units, Max	14%
pH (mean daily min)	7.9 pH Units	6.5 pH Units, Min	0%
Turbidity (mean daily max)	104 NTU[e]	< 50 NTU over background (instantaneous) < 25 for 10 consecutive days	Insufficient data
E. coli	46.7 MPN/100 ml	< 406 *E. coli*/100 ml	0%
Fecal Coliform	22 MPN/100ML	<500 cfu/100 ml	0%

*MDMT – Maximum Daily Maximum Temperature, **MDAT – Maximum Daily Average Temperature, [a] Mix of TMDLs and criteria for cold water life designation, [b] Proportion of samples above water quality standard [c] Poor data quality precludes reporting, [d] Criteria for cold water life designation, [e] Mean daily max based on 2 months of data due to poor data quality

0-5% exceedance	
5-25% exceedance	
>25% exceedance	

Acknowledgments

Funding for this project was provided through the National Park Service Natural Resource Challenge and the Servicewide Inventory and Monitoring Program.

Introduction and Background

Water resources have been identified as a high priority vital sign for the Upper Columbia Basin Network (UCBN). These resources are used by many riparian, migratory, and terrestrial organisms in the Network, and have intrinsic value as places of natural beauty and recreation (Garrett et al. 2007). Reflecting this priority, the Water Resources Division (WRD) of the NPS provides a separate source of funding each fiscal year to the UUCBN to accomplish water quality monitoring. In June 2011 the UCBN began its first year of integrated water quality monitoring in Jim Ford Creek and its second year in Lapwai Creek at Nez Perce National Historical Park (NEPE).

Water resources in the semi-arid West have been strongly affected by human activity, and many UCBN streams and rivers are listed by states as impaired for one or more parameters. Most UCBN water bodies and many aquatic resources such as migratory fish are strongly influenced by activities in the larger watersheds outside park boundaries. Understanding the current status of freshwater ecosystems will help guide management and restoration efforts, and provide insight into ecosystem change in a landscape with a shifting climate and dynamic human influences.

During the process of prioritizing vital signs to monitor in UCBN parks in 2005, water quality was identified as a high priority vital sign (Garrett et al. 2007). When asked what aspects of water quality were important to monitor, resource managers identified the sampling of macroinvertebrate assemblages within UCBN water bodies as the top water quality monitoring priority. Secondary priorities included baseline sampling of water chemistry parameters, characterization of channel morphology, and information on water quantity. Channel morphology and riparian vegetation are addressed in separate monitoring protocols which were also implemented at NEPE in 2011.

The objectives of the UCBN Integrated Water Quality Monitoring Protocol are documenting the aquatic macroinvertebrate assemblage composition and baseline water chemistry parameters. Aquatic macroinvertebrate assemblages have strong effects on freshwater ecosystem processes and represent an important trophic linkage between primary producers and fishes. Measures of macroinvertebrate assemblage composition and structure have been frequently used as water quality indicators because these assemblages integrate the effects of point and non-point source pollutants over spatial-temporal scales and can be used to answer many management questions. Also, macroinvertebrates are more cost-effective to sample than other biota or many water chemistry parameters.

Water chemistry and temperature have strong effects on aquatic biota. Consequently, direct and indirect human alteration of stream water quality is associated with altered biotic communities and ecosystem processes. Because of the direct relationship between water chemistry and biota, water chemistry is typically a central component of any water quality monitoring program. More recently, monitoring of stream water temperatures has increased in the Pacific Northwest, because of concerns over cold-water fish habitat (primarily salmonid fishes), the recognized influence of land- and water-use on stream temperature regime, and the need for baseline temperature information to monitor the effects of climate change. National Park Service (NPS) Water Resource Division (WRD) has identified a suite of four "core water quality parameters":

temperature, specific conductance, pH, and dissolved oxygen, which are critical to understanding baseline conditions in aquatic habitats. The UCBN added turbidity as a parameter to measure because turbidity is listed as a source of impairment in several UCBN park streams.

Well articulated desired future condition statements have not yet been developed for water quality in UCBN parks. However, the mission statements for the NPS as a whole and for the individual parks clearly state the intent "to conserve unimpaired the natural and cultural resources and values of the national park system for the enjoyment of this and future generations" (NPS 1999). Water quality is a particularly important resource with nationally recognized merit. It is assumed that desired future conditions for all UCBN parks will include clean streams, rivers, and lakes free of human health concerns that provide visitors with recreational and scenic experiences. Monitoring macroinvertebrate assemblage composition and structure, and core water quality parameters will directly measure the water characteristics most important to park mission, visitor experience, and desired future conditions.

Objectives

The overarching programmatic goal of the UCBN integrated water quality monitoring program is to obtain information that will aid in informed management decisions pertaining to improved water quality within UCBN parks. Park managers have committed to improving the water quality of impaired waters by adopting the NPS Government Performance Results Act (GPRA) goal (Ia4) that streams and rivers managed by NPS will meet State and Federal water quality standards (NPS 2000).

Given this goal, it should be noted that in 2010 Jim Ford Creek was listed as a category 4A water for temperature, sedimentation/siltation, fecal coliform, and nutrient eutrophication. A category 4A means that it has a pollution problem, but has total maximum daily loads (TMDL) being actively implemented to remedy issues. In addition, in 1998 Lapwai Creek was on the 303(d) list for pollution problems related to: (bacteria, flow alteration, habitat alteration, nutrients, sediment, dissolved oxygen and temperature. Since that time it has been listed as a category 3 stream meaning that it is considered an unassessed water (see study area description below for more information).

Given the lack of available data on water quality in UCBN parks, the following fundamental questions drive much of the UCBN's inquiry into water quality:

- Are the core water quality parameters of streams in the UCBN with established Total Maximum Daily Loads (TMDLs) selected for sampling improving over time?
- What is the status and long-term trend of core water quality parameters (temperature, pH, conductivity, dissolved oxygen, and turbidity) in UCBN streams selected for sampling?
- What is the status and long term trend in aquatic macroinvertebrate abundance and assemblage composition in selected UCBN streams?
- Do aquatic macroinvertebrate assemblages sampled within UCBN streams indicate polluted or otherwise impaired water quality?
- Do aquatic macroinvertebrate assemblages sampled within UCBN streams indicate "pristine" or "reference" conditions according to regional criteria established by the (Environmental Protection Agency (EPA) and the states of Idaho, Oregon, Montana, and Washington?

In light of these questions and the broader goals outlined above, water quality monitoring in the UCBN addresses the following specific measurable monitoring objectives:

- Determine status and long term trend in key water quality parameters for selected streams within UCBN park units.
- Determine status and trend in aquatic macroinvertebrate abundance, assemblage composition, and functional feeding group composition in wadeable streams within the UCBN.

Study Area

Jim Ford Creek- Nez Perce National Historical Park (NEPE), Weippe Prairie

The segment of Jim Ford Creek within the park is in the lower Clearwater River drainage in Hydrologic Unit Code (HUC 6)170603060401 (United States Geologic Survey [USGS]), Upper Jim Ford Creek subwatershed, in Clearwater County, Idaho (Figure 2, Appendix B). The Weippe Prairie watershed is approximately 142 square km (54 square miles) and consists of several land cover types (Erixson et al. 2010). According to Erixson, et al. 2010, Weippe's watershed is primarily tree dominated vegetation (*Abies grandis, Pseudotsuga menziesii, Pinus ponderosa*) (67.9%), with smaller land cover components consisting of herbaceous vegetation (6.3%), shrub-dominated vegetation (6.4%), and agriculture (6.3%).

Designated beneficial uses for Jim Ford Creek include: cold water biota, primary contact recreation, secondary contact recreation, and agricultural water supply (ID DEQ, Nez Perce Tribe EPA 2000). The primary threats to water resources in Weippe Prairie are: point and non-point discharge from upstream sources, agriculture, logging, grazing, recreation, and historic landuse (Garrett et al. 2007). In 2010, Jim Ford Creek was listed as a category 4A impaired water for temperature, sedimentation/siltation, fecal coliform, and nutrient eutrophication (ID DEQ 2011). The category 4A designation means that it has a pollution problem, but has total maximum daily loads (TMDL) being actively implemented to reduce pollution. The current TMDLs can be found in Idaho Department of Environmental Quality(ID DEQ), Nez Perce Tribe EPA 2000. Additional information about Jim Ford Creek can be found in Jim Ford Creek Water Quality Monitoring Report 2003-2004 (Clark 2005) and Natural Resource Condition Assessment: Nez Perce National Historical Park (Erixson et al. 2010).

The Hydrolab was deployed approximately 200 m downstream of the bridge (Larson or Prairie Road) over Jim Ford Creek (Figure 1, Figure 3 and Appendix A). This location was chosen primarily due to adequate water depth during late summer months. The macroinvertebrate sample reaches along Jim Ford Creek coincide with the stream channel characteristics and riparian condition monitoring reaches (see Appendix C for GPS waypoint).

Figure 1. Jim Ford Creek looking downstream towards water quality monitoring station #01. Just beyond the hawthorn tree on right bank.

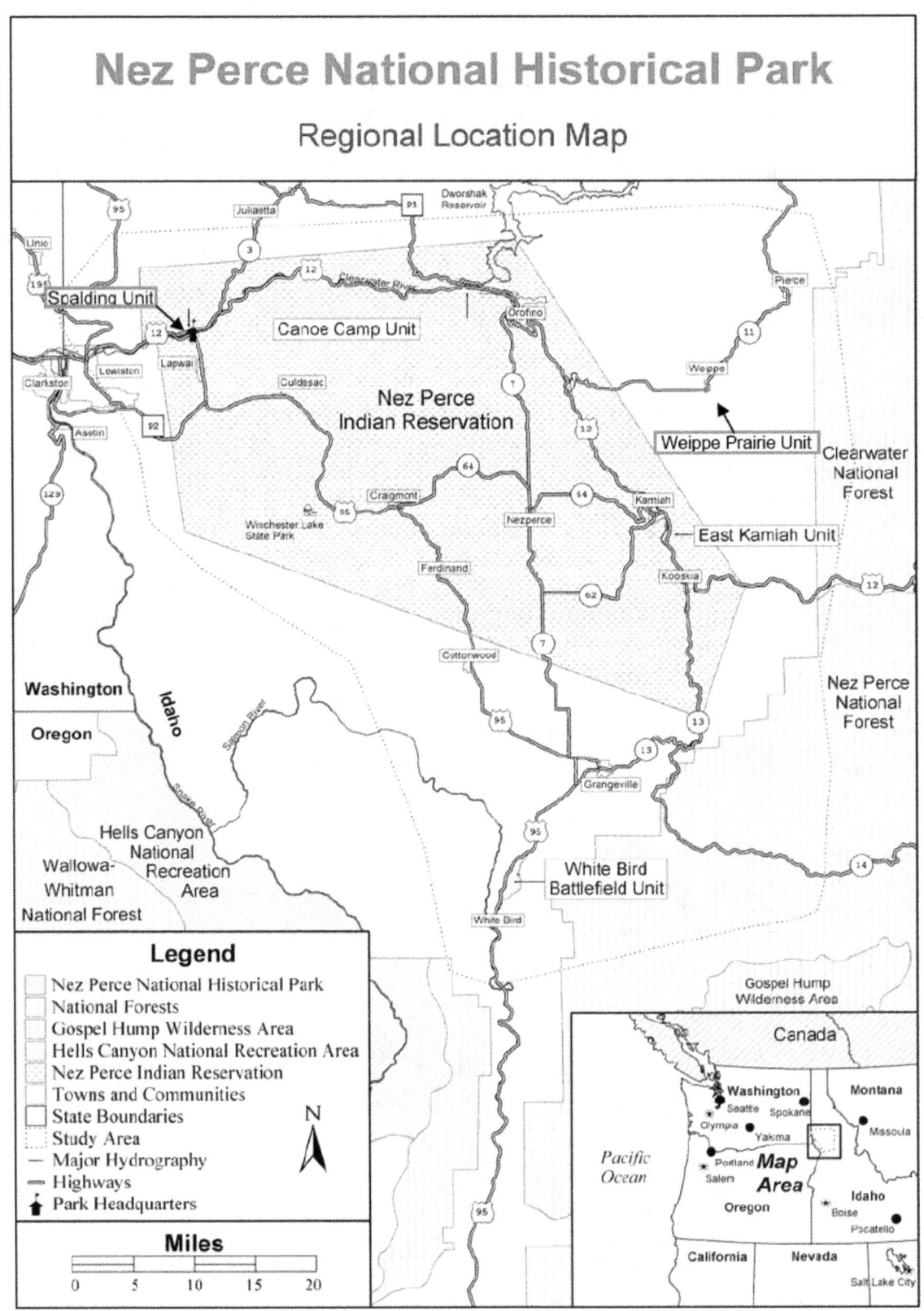

Figure 2. Nez Perce National Historical Park regional map (NPS 1997). Note that monitoring occurred in both the Spalding and Weippe Prairie Units.

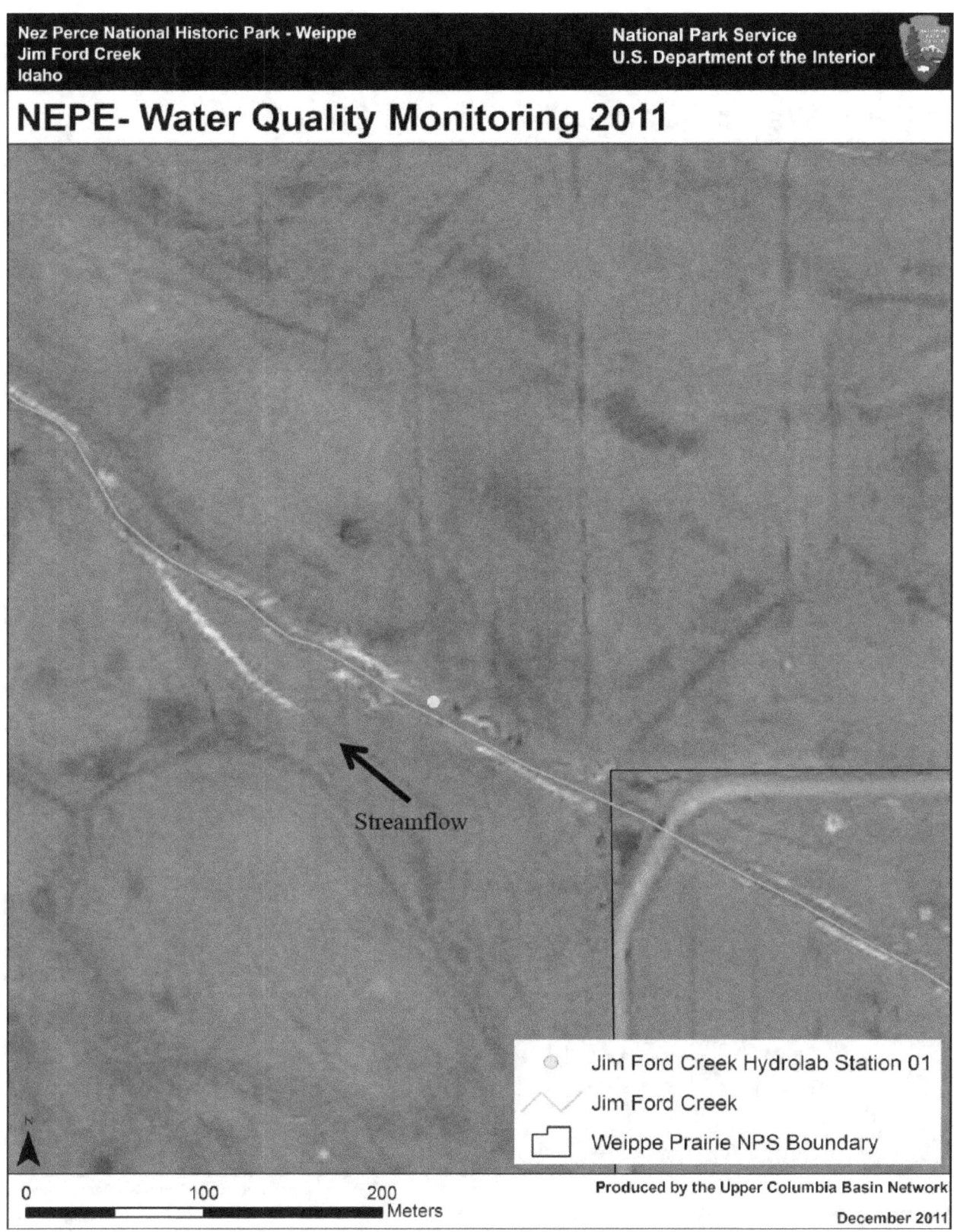

Figure 3. Water quality monitoring location in Jim Ford Creek 2011.

Figure 4. Water quality monitoring location in Lapwai Creek 2011.

Lapwai Creek- Nez Perce National Historical Park (NEPE), Spalding

Lapwai Creek is in the lower Clearwater River drainage in Hydrologic Unit Code (HUC 6) 170603061304 (United States Geologic Survey [USGS]), Lower Lapwai Creek subwatershed, in Nez Perce County, Idaho (Figure 2 and Appendix B). The Spalding watershed is approximately 305 square km (118 square miles) and consists of several land cover types (Erixson et al. 2010). According to Erixson, et al. 2010, Spalding's watershed consists of the following land cover types: agriculture (52.9%), shrub dominated vegetation (20.4%), herbaceous vegetation (12.6%) and developed areas (i.e., City of Lewiston) (9.7%). For a description of each landcover type see Erixson et al. 2010.

Designated beneficial uses for Lapwai Creek (from Sweetwater Creek to mouth) include: cold water biota and primary contact recreation ID Admin Code 2011, 58.01.02.120.08 (through 5/3/03). Threats to water resources in NEPE have been listed as: point and non-point discharge from upstream sources, agriculture, logging, grazing, recreation, highway runoff and urbanization. (Garrett et al. 2007). In 1998, Lapwai Creek was on the 303(d) list for pollution problems related to: (bacteria, flow alteration, habitat alteration, nutrients, sediment, dissolved oxygen and temperature. In 2010, Lapwai Creek was listed as a category 3 (unassessed) water by the state of Idaho meaning that it had not been assessed or had insufficient data to determine if water quality standards were attained (ID DEQ 2011). The 2010 integrated report also lists Lapwai Creek as a Tribal water meaning that Idaho DEQ does not make 303(d) listing judgments or lead the development of TMDLs. Development of TMDLs depends on the Environmental Protection Agency (EPA) and the Tribe. In effect, the reason Lapwai Creek (Sweetwater Creek to Mouth) is listed as a category 3 stream is due to its "tribal water" designation (ID DEQ 2011). Additional information on Lapwai Creek can be found in the Lapwai Creek Aquatic Assessment (Cichosz et al. 2001), the Lapwai Creek Watershed Ecological Restoration Strategy (Richardson et al. 2009), UCBN Integrated Water Quality Annual Report 2008 NEPE and WHMI (Starkey 2009) and the Natural Resource Condition Assessment: Nez Perce National Historical Park (Erixson et al. 2010).

The Hydrolab was deployed in the same location as in 2008, approximately 100 meters downstream from the railroad bridge (Figures 4 and 5, Appendix A). This location was chosen due to logistical considerations, adequate water depth, and to avoid placement of equipment near creek access points.

The macroinvertebrate sample reach on Lapwai Creek coincides with the stream channel characteristics and riparian condition monitoring reach (see Appendix C for GPS waypoint).

Figure 5. Lapwai Creek looking upstream from water quality monitoring station #01.

Methods

Water Chemistry

Continuous water quality monitors (HACH, MS5 Hydrolabs) were deployed from June 17th to October 5th in Jim Ford Creek, and from June 22nd to November 3rd in Lapwai Creek at index sites to estimate the status, variability, and long-term trends in core parameters. The core parameters measured were water temperature, dissolved oxygen, pH, specific conductance, and turbidity. These core parameters were measured hourly and the instrument serviced monthly throughout the deployment period. Each monitor was deployed in a location that was representative of conditions in the park, logistically feasible to access, and relatively secure from vandalism and high flows. A cross-section survey was conducted to aid in the determination of Hydrolab site selection. For more information on the UCBN water chemistry sampling design see Starkey et al. (2008). It should be noted that monitoring on Jim Ford Creek ended in October 2011 rather than November due to the failure of the dissolved oxygen sensor. In addition, a gap in Jim Ford monitoring occurred from August 18th to September 1st when Hydrolab #064 was sent to the Hach Company for repair of the dissolved oxygen sensor. This instrument was re-installed on September 1st. A gap in monitoring also occurred on Lapwai Creek between September 14th and September 27th when Hydrolab #054 was sent to the Hach Company for repair of the turbidity sensor. The instrument was re-installed on September 27th.

Quality Assurance/Quality Control (QA/QC):

Quality assurance and quality control for multiprobe data collection are covered in detail in SOP #12 (Starkey et al. 2008). Basic procedures adhere to the guidelines established in Part B lite (Irwin 2008); the National Coastal Assessment Quality Assurance Project Plan 2001-2004 (U.S. EPA 2001); the Laboratory Methods Manual-Estuaries, Volume 1: Biological and Physical Analyses (U.S. EPA 1995); and Rapid Bioassessment Protocols for Use in Streams and Wadeable Rivers (Barbour et al. 1999).

General quality assurance and quality control methods for UCBN water quality multiprobe calibration and data downloads include the following:

- Representative multiprobe sample locations are determined by using a cross-section and stream segment survey. Each site is re-assessed for representativeness at the start and end each sample year.

- The UCBN follows pre-established maximum acceptable differences for field instrument calibration and QC checks. If the multiprobe readings are outside of the maximum acceptable differences, the multiprobe is removed for non-routine maintenance.

- When calibrating the multiprobe, values of known standard solutions are measured pre and post calibration, to help determine if the instrument's measurements have "drifted." In addition, repeated measures of these solutions are used to determine the repeatability of multiprobe measures.

- All multiprobe data is visually checked for outliers and QC issues immediately following the download of data. QC issues indicated by the data may include: wiper parking, defective sensors, power supply problems, and other anomalies affecting data quality.

- Quantitative and qualitative terms that describe how accurate data need to be in order to meet project objectives are discussed in detail in SOP #12 Starkey et al. 2008 and Appendix D in this report. NPS WRD lists the following data quality objectives as necessary for water chemistry data: target population, representativeness, completeness, data comparability, measurement sensitivity and detection limits, measurement precision as repeatability, and measurement systematic error/bias.

More detailed QA/QC for water quality multiprobes is contained in SOP #6 and 12, Starkey et al. 2008.

Discharge
Water discharge was determined by data available from the United States Geological Survey (USGS) real time gauging sites. For Lapwai Creek, the closest gage is near the town of Lapwai, ID, #13342450. This data was used to aid in the interpretation of continuous water chemistry data collected June – November 2011. No USGS gauging station exists on Jim Ford Creek.

Macroinvertebrates
On both Jim Ford and Lapwai Creeks, macroinvertebrates were collected at designated sample reaches (6 on Jim Ford Creek, 1 on Lapwai Creek) by the United States Forest Service-PACFISH/INFISH Biological Opinion (PIBO) Effectiveness Monitoring Program during the assessment of stream channel characteristics. This assessment was completed as part of the UCBNs stream channel characteristics monitoring protocol. Macroinvertebrates were collected from 8 fast water habitats (riffles, runs) in each sample reach. These 8 samples were combined for a single composite sample per reach. For more information on the PIBO macroinvertebrate sampling design see Heitke et al. (2008).

Coliform
At the request of the park, coliform samples were collected to determine baseline counts for total coliform, fecal coliform and *E. coli*. Note that coliform sampling is not routinely performed as part of the Integrated Water Quality Protocol. Samples were drawn from both Jim Ford and Lapwai Creeks near the water quality monitoring stations on August 24th, 2011. Samples were chilled and transported to Anatek Labs in Moscow, ID for analysis.

Results

Jim Ford Creek- Weippe Prairie

Water Chemistry:

Cross Section Survey:
A cross section survey was conducted at the proposed multiprobe deployment location to evaluate if the site was reasonably representative of stream conditions throughout the park. As suggested by the water resource division the UCBN judges overall representativeness primarily on the basis of specific conductance (Starkey et al. 2008).

The 2011 deployment location provided adequate water depth throughout the field season, was easily accessible, and was away from heavily trafficked access points. There are limited other deployment locations along the creek due to frequent visitor use and lack of pools.

A one way analysis of variance (ANOVA) test was conducted to evaluate representativeness (R v2.12.0). Results of the ANOVA showed that there was a significant difference for specific conductance among the transects and the deployment location in July $F(4,41)=8.21$, $p < 0.05$ and in September $F(4,41)= 2347.2$, $p < 0.05$.

To determine where the difference in representativeness occurred, a post hoc Tukey's test was conducted (R v2.12.0). Relative to specific conductance, results of the Tukey's test for the cross section conducted in July indicates that the deployment location was significantly different from transects 1, 2, 3, and 4 (Figure 6). Results of the Tukey's test for the cross section conducted in September also indicates that the deployment location was significantly different from transects 1, 2, 3, and 4 (Figure 7).

While both cross section surveys indicate the monitoring station may not have been representative of conditions downstream, both physical and hydrological factors limit the utility of these surveys. During both surveys, surface flow had ceased and each cross section transect was within a distinct isolated pool of varying depth. Specific conductance may have varied between pools due to differential rates of evaporation between pools. The second factor influencing the utility of this data was that during each cross section survey the substrate (very fine clay particles) was disturbed and remained suspended during the cross section due to the lack of surface flow. Given that the monitoring location was within the largest and deepest pool in the park, it represents the best/only location suitable for permanent deployment. If a cross section was completed during periods of persistent surface flow (difficult due to water depth) the results would likely indicate that the deployment location is representative of conditions throughout the park.

In the future, this location will likely remain the best option for long term deployment of the water quality monitor.

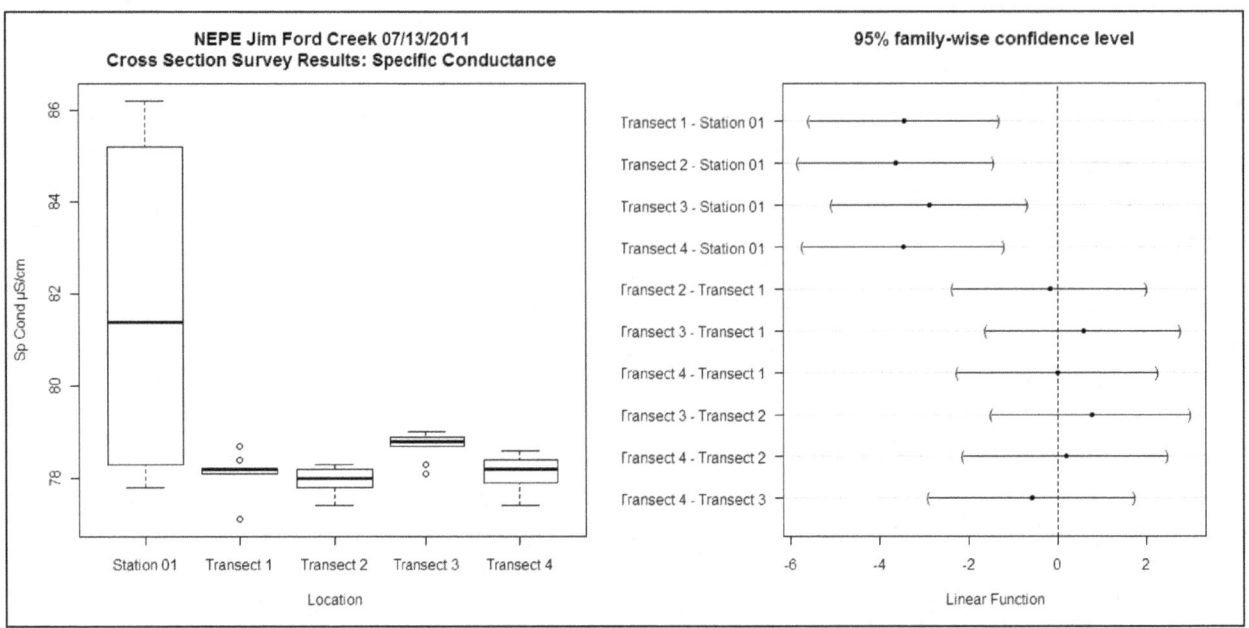

Figure 6. July 2011 cross section survey of Jim Ford Creek, box plot of specific conductance and plot of 95% family-wise confidence level.
Note that "Station 01" is the location of multiprobe deployment and transects progress downstream (1-4).

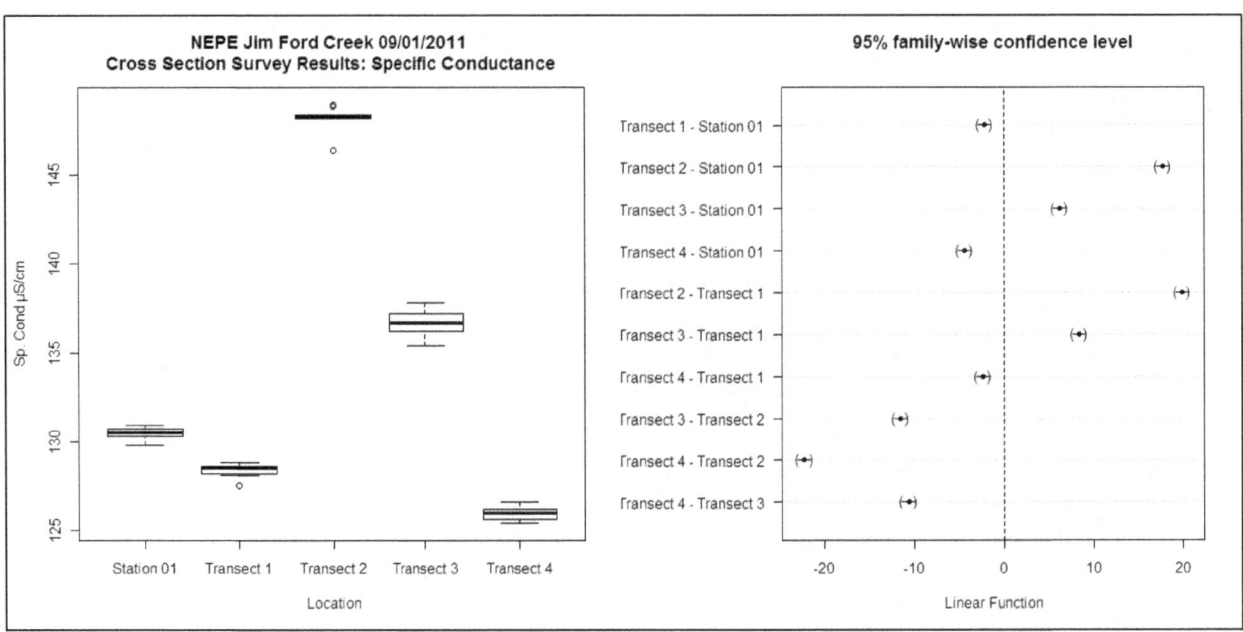

Figure 7. September 2011 cross section survey of Jim Ford Creek, box plot of specific conductance and plot of 95% family-wise confidence level.
Note that "Station 01" is the location of multiprobe deployment and transects progress upstream (1-4).

Status:

Condition of core water quality parameters along with the corresponding Idaho DEQ regulatory threshold are given in Table 1. The primary concern is elevated water temperatures and their effect on native fish and other cold water biota. Each parameter is discussed in further detail below.

Table 1. Vital sign summary table for water chemistry in the Jim Ford Creek June-October, 2011

Jim Ford Creek Water Chemistry Summary 2011

Measure	Current Condition (June-October, 2011)	State DEQ Thresholds [a]	% Exceedance [b]
Temperature (*MDMT, **MDAT)	* MDMT= 22.26 °C ** MDAT= 21.68 °C	*MDMT<22 °C **MDAT<19 °C	5 % 42%
Specific conductance (mean)	108.7 µS/cm	N/A	N/A
Dissolved oxygen (mean daily min)	6.6 mg/l	> 6.0 mg/l	1 %
pH (mean daily max)	7.36 pH Units	9.0 pH Units, Max	0%
pH (mean daily min)	7.12 pH Units	6.5 pH Units, Min	0%
Turbidity (mean daily max)	--[c]	< 50 NTU over background (instantaneous) < 25 for 10 consecutive days	Insufficient data
E. coli	33.5 MPN/100 ml	< 406 E. coli/100 ml	0%
Fecal Coliform	33 MPN/100 ml	<500 cfu/100 ml	0%

*MDMT – Maximum Daily Maximum Temperature, **MDAT – Maximum Daily Average Temperature,
[a] Mix of TMDLs and criteria for cold water life designation [b] Proportion of samples above water quality standard [c] Poor data quality precludes reporting, see turbidity section below for more details.

0-5% exceedance	
5-25% exceedance	
>25% exceedance	

- *Temperature:*

  The maximum daily maximum temperature (MDMT) exceeded 22.0 °C in 5% of observations and the maximum daily average temperature (MDAT) exceeded 19 °C in 42% of observations. Our data reinforces basin-wide temperature concerns as discussed in the Jim Ford Creek Total Maximum Daily Load (TMDL) (ID DEQ, Nez Perce Tribe EPA 2000). Figure 8 shows the daily maximum and mean daily temperatures in Jim Ford Creek from June-October 2011. Table 2 lists the data rating/grade for each deployment period (monthly interval). These standard USGS ratings are based on the degree of sensor fouling and drift encountered during each deployment period (Wagner et al. 2006; Starkey et al. 2008).

  Water temperatures are of particular interest in Jim Ford Creek, given that its designated use includes cold water biota. Implications of elevated water temperatures may include decreased salmonid recruitment, decreased salmonid health, and potential shifts in fish and benthic macroinvertebrate communities (Vannote and Sweeney 1980; McCullough 1999). It is also important to note that elevated water temperatures have the capacity to reduce the total concentration of dissolved oxygen (i.e., there is an inverse relationship between water temperature and dissolved oxygen; Figure 10), thereby impacting aquatic biota.

15

Maintaining water temperatures suitable for naturally occurring species in Jim Ford Creek will depend on riparian and stream channel conditions basin-wide. For this reason cooperation with other agencies, stakeholders, and adjacent landowners will be critical for improving water temperature.

- *Specific Conductance:*
  Specific conductance ranged from 46.0 to 156.9 µS/cm, with an average specific conductance of 108.7 µS/cm. The steady increase in specific conductance shown in Figure 9 reflects the cessation of surface flow and subsequent drop in water level associated with evaporation throughout the summer. Table 3 shows the data rating/grade for each deployment period (monthly interval). These standard USGS ratings are based on the degree of sensor fouling and drift encountered during each deployment period (Wagner et al. 2006; Starkey et al. 2008). The specific conductance data grade of "good" was due to a combination of fouling and sensor drift.

Corrections that have been applied to the specific conductance data are listed in Appendix E.

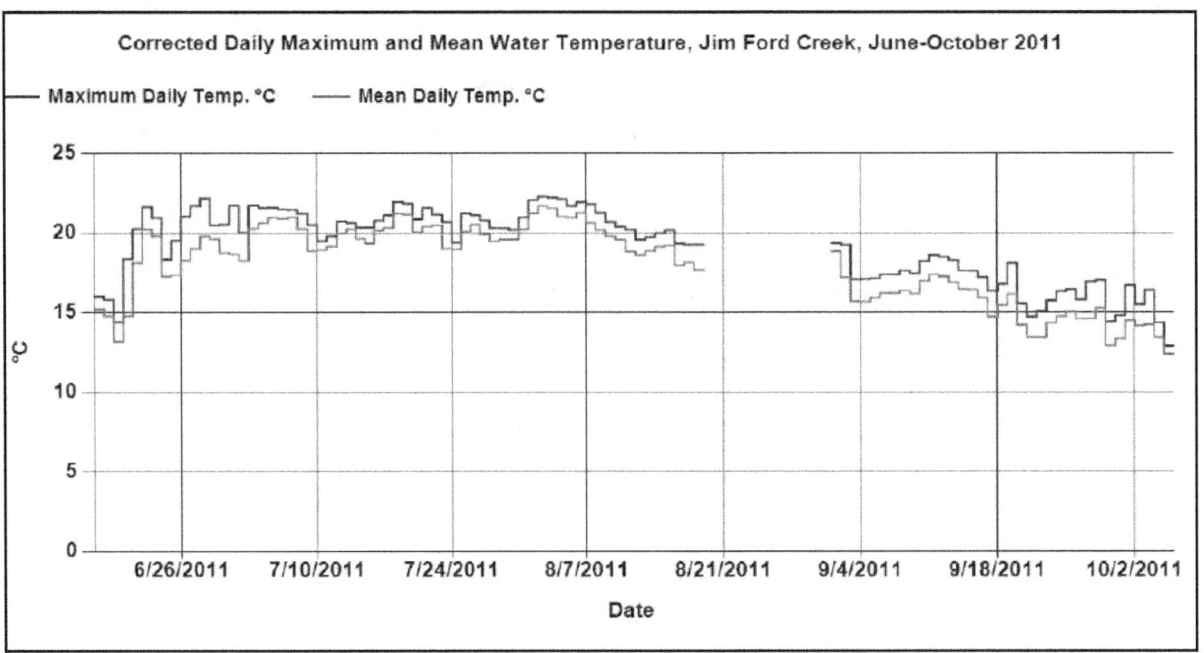

Figure 8. Daily maximum and mean temperature in Jim Ford Creek, NEPE, 2011.

Table 2. Data grade/rating for water temperature each deployment period June-October 2011 in Jim Ford Creek, NEPE.

Temperature Data Grade/Rating	From UTC-07:00	To UTC-07:00
GOOD	6/17/2011 14:00	7/14/2011 9:00
FAIR	7/14/2011 17:00	8/18/2011 9:00
EXCELLENT	9/1/2011 13:00	10/5/2011 9:00

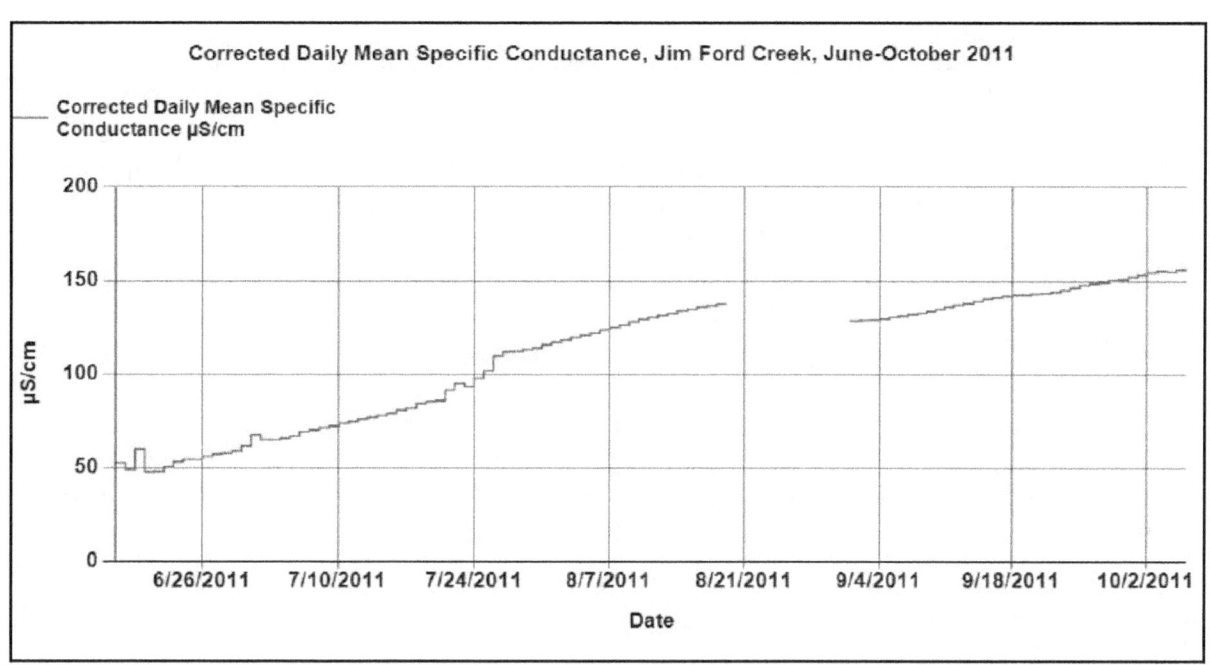

Figure 9. Corrected daily mean specific conductance in Jim Ford Creek, NEPE, 2011.

Table 3. Data grade/rating for specific conductance each deployment period June-October 2011 in Jim Ford Creek, NEPE.

Specific Conductance Data Grade/Rating	From UTC-07:00	To UTC-07:00
EXCELLENT	6/17/2011 14:00	7/14/2011 9:00
EXCELLENT	7/14/2011 17:00	8/18/2011 9:00
GOOD	9/1/2011 13:00	10/5/2011 9:00

- *Dissolved Oxygen:*
  Mean daily minimum dissolved oxygen was 6.6 mg/L and dipped below the regulatory threshold (6.0 mg/L) during 1% of observations. As expected, minimum dissolved oxygen levels generally corresponded to maximum water temperatures. Figure 10 shows the daily minimum dissolved oxygen and maximum temperatures in Jim Ford Creek from June-October 2011. Table 4 shows the data rating/grade for each deployment period (monthly interval). These standard USGS ratings are based on the degree of sensor fouling and drift encountered during each deployment period (Wagner et al. 2006; Starkey et al. 2008). Data grades of "poor" and "unusable" were due to heavy fouling and sensor failure. Corrections applied to the dissolved oxygen data are listed in Appendix E.

  The nutrient and dissolved oxygen TMDL for Jim Ford Creek are combined due to the assumption that low dissolved oxygen levels are generally being driven by excess instream nutrients (nitrogen and phosphorous) (ID DEQ, Nez Perce Tribe EPA 2000). While the UCBN's monitoring did not directly measure nutrients, the dissolved oxygen data suggests that eutrophication may play a minor role in depressing dissolved oxygen levels in the portion of Jim Ford Creek within the Weippie Prairie unit.

  While our monitoring did not indicate frequent exceedance of the water quality standard, even infrequent low dissolved oxygen can be a threat to the native aquatic biota, especially when coupled with elevated water temperatures. Minimum dissolved oxygen levels can likely be increased if water temperatures are reduced via stream shading.

- *pH:*
  The minimum and maximum pH (6.8 and 7.8 respectively) were never outside the acceptable regulatory thresholds of 6.5-9.0 pH units and the median (7.2 pH units) was well within this range. Figure 11 shows the daily maximum, minimum, and median pH in Jim Ford Creek from June-October 2011. Table 5 shows the data rating/grade for each deployment period (monthly interval). These standard USGS ratings are based on the degree of sensor fouling and drift encountered during each deployment period (Wagner et al. 2006; Starkey et al. 2008). Data grades less than "excellent" were due to a combination of sensor fouling and drift. Corrections applied to the pH data are listed in Appendix E.

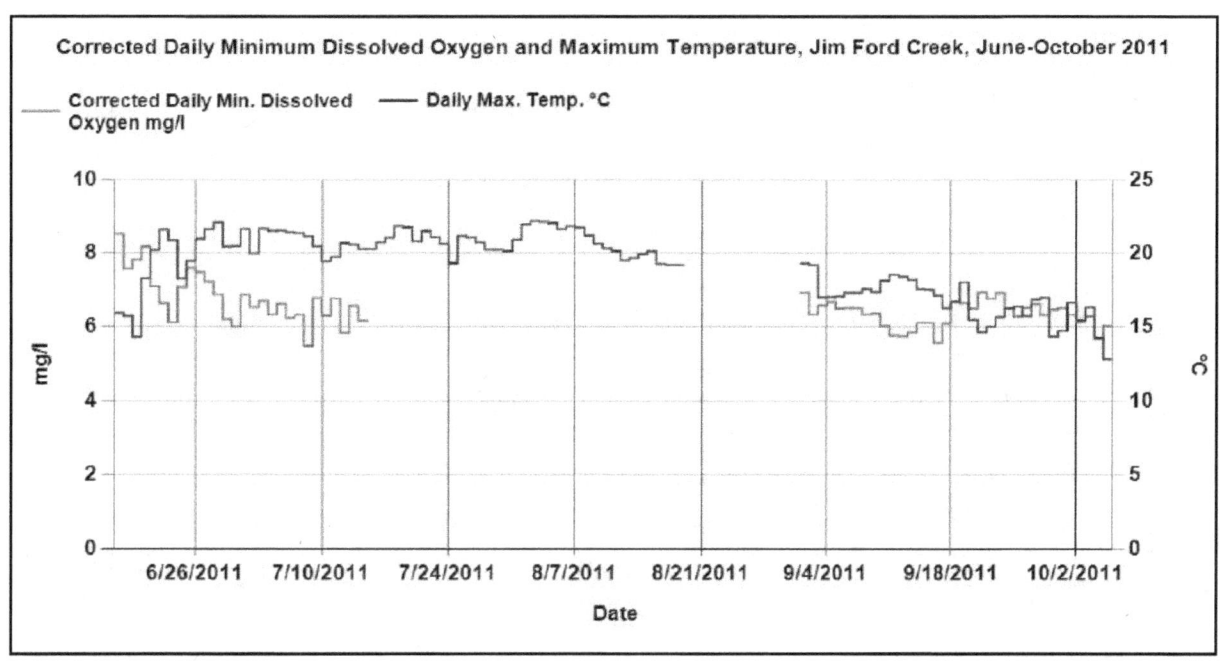

Figure 10. Corrected daily minimum dissolved oxygen and daily maximum temperature in Jim Ford Creek, NEPE, 2011. Note that "unusable" data is not displayed in the graph (7/14/2011 to 8/18/2011).

Table 4. Data grade/rating for dissolved oxygen each deployment period June-October 2011 in Jim Ford Creek, NEPE.

Dissolved Oxygen Data Grade/Rating	From UTC-07:00	To UTC-07:00
POOR	6/17/2011 14:00	7/14/2011 9:00
UNUSABLE	7/14/2011 17:00	8/18/2011 9:00
GOOD	9/1/2011 13:00	10/5/2011 9:00

19

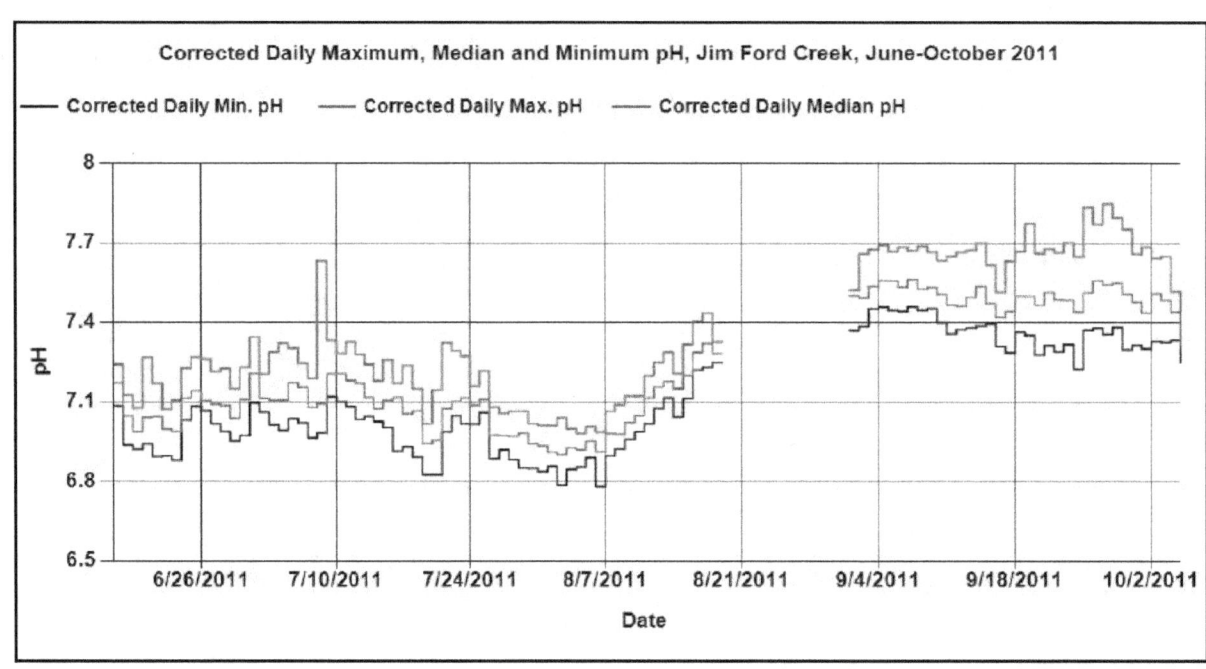

Figure 11. Corrected daily maximum, minimum, and median pH in Jim Ford Creek, NEPE, 2011. Note that the maximum and minimum regulatory thresholds were never exceeded (6.5, 9.0 pH units).

Table 5. Data grade/rating for pH each deployment period June-October 2011 in Jim Ford Creek, NEPE.

pH Data Grade/Rating	From UTC-07:00	To UTC-07:00
GOOD	6/17/2011 14:00	7/14/2011 9:00
GOOD	7/14/2011 17:00	8/18/2011 9:00
GOOD	9/1/2011 13:00	10/5/2011 9:00

- *Turbidity:*

  Prior to discussion about turbidity in Jim Ford Creek (Figure 12), it should be noted that conclusions based on this data are limited due to extremely poor/unusable data quality (Table 6). Sensor fouling due to sediment and sensor drift (possibly associated with the dissolved oxygen sensor failure) were the primary factors influencing data quality. It is important to note that the method detection limit (MDL) for this sensor was 0.2 NTU and the minimum level of quantitation (ML) was 0.53 NTU (Appendix D). Figure 12 shows the raw (uncorrected) daily mean turbidity in the Jim Ford Creek from June-October 2011. Raw values were graphed because the program used to manage the water quality data (AQUAIRUS) will only graph corrected data if it has a data grade better than "unusable" (i.e., Poor–Excellent). Corrections that were applied to turbidity data are listed in Appendix E.

  Data indicates that turbidity ranged from <0.2 to 43 NTU. However, due to poor data quality and lack of historic data for this site the UCBN is unable to determine if conditions exceeded the state standard. Regulatory thresholds for turbidity state that it should be "< 50 NTU over background (instantaneous) and < 25 NTU for 10 consecutive days." Although conclusions are limited based on the quality of data collected in 2011 it is likely that Jim Ford Creek does experience relatively high levels of turbidity in part due to historic/current land use and historic stream channel modifications.

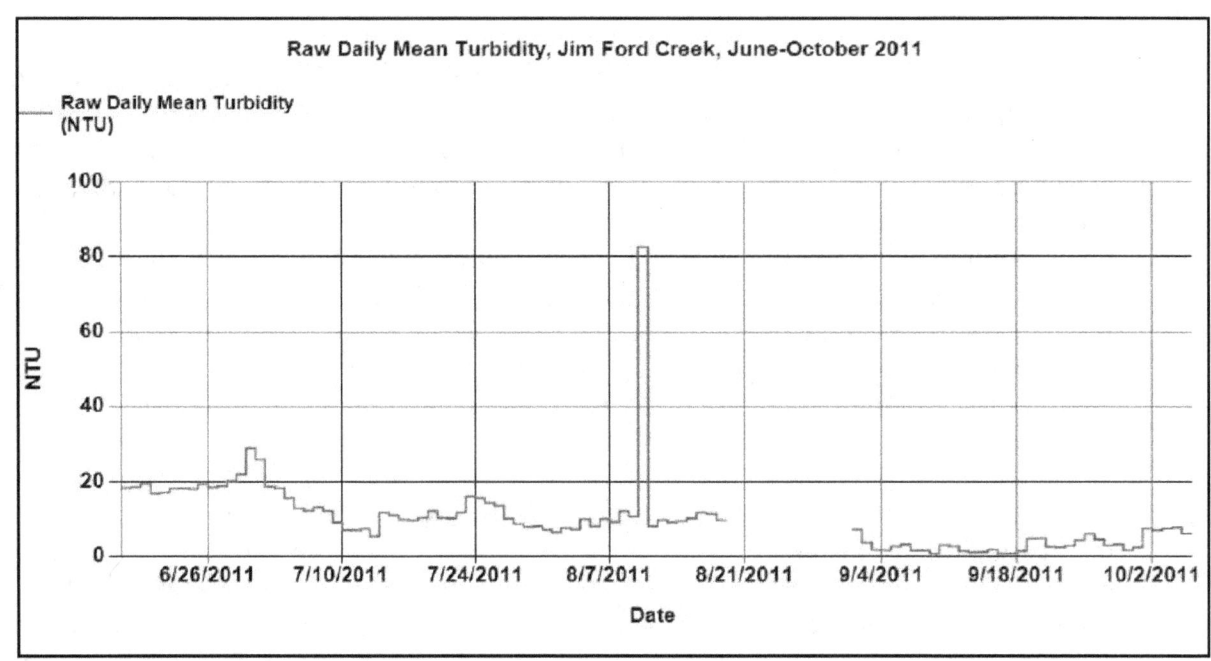

Figure 12. Raw daily mean turbidity in Jim Ford Creek, NEPE, 2011.
Note that the un-usable data grades (blue) presented in table 6 were primarily due to severe fouling.

Table 6. Data grade/rating for turbidity each deployment period June-October 2011 in Jim Ford Creek, NEPE.

Turbidity Data Grade/Rating	From UTC-07:00	To UTC-07:00
UNUSABLE	6/17/2011 14:00	7/14/2011 9:00
UNUSABLE	7/14/2011 17:00	8/18/2011 9:00
UNUSABLE	9/1/2011 13:00	10/5/2011 9:00

Macroinvertebrates

Status:

Prior to discussion about the status of macroinvertebrates in Jim Ford Creek, it should be noted the United States Forest Service- PACFISH/INFISH Biological Opinion (PIBO) did not find a single benthic macroinvertebrate in one of the 3 reaches it sampled. The other 3 sample reaches were dry at the time of sample collection (8/18/2011). The results below are for the 2 sample reaches containing macroinvertebrates.

The Hilsenhoff Biotic Index (HBI), which summarizes pollution tolerances of the macroinvertebrate taxa within the sample, indicates that Jim Ford Creek has "fairly substantial [organic] pollution likely" and "fair" water quality (HBI= 5.48, and 5.44) (Hilsenhoff 1987, 1988). HBI values generally increase (HBI ranges from 0.0 to 10.0) as nutrient enrichment increases. While HBI is most sensitive to organic pollution, it may also respond to sediment loading, low dissolved oxygen and elevated water temperatures. The US Forest Service (USFS) community tolerance quotient was 103 and 108 and indicates that Jim Ford Creek's benthic macroinvertebrate community is severely impaired. Values of the USFS tolerance quotient range from 20 to just over100, with lower values indicating better water quality.

In a single sample reach, the maximum number of Ephemeroptera, Plecoptera, Trichoptera (EPT) taxa was 2; there were a maximum of 2 long lived taxa; and the dominate family was Chironomidae (non-biting midges). These data along with the tolerance indices listed above suggest that Jim Ford Creek is impaired. Causes of impairment may be tied to elevated water temperatures, or lack of summer stream flow. At the time this report was written, stream channel data from the UCBN's stream channel characteristics monitoring protocol were not available. However, these data may indicate that physical factors (substrate armoring, sediment loading, bank erosion, etc.) are negatively impacting benthic assemblages.

The observed to expected ratio (OE) for both sample reaches was 0.18. However, a condition rating (i.e., good, fair, poor) could not be assigned because both samples contained fewer than the required number of organisms for the model (>200). See Table 23 and Appendix F for additional summary metrics.

Table 7. Vital sign summary table for benthic macroinvertebrates in Jim Ford Creek, 2011.
PIBO stations 3117, 3119, and 3120 were not sampled due to a dry stream channel.
Note that the entire macroinvertebrate taxa and metrics lists can be found in Appendix F and G.

Jim Ford Creek Macroinvertebrate Summary August 2011			
PIBO Station	**3115**	**3116**	**3118**
Sample ID	**147158**	**147159**	**147160**
Richness*	0	7	5
Shannon's Diversity*	0	1.23	1.02
Simpson's Diversity*	0	0.60	0.55
Evenness*	0	0.63	0.63
# of EPT Taxa*	0	2	0
Dominant Family	--	Chironomidae	Chironomidae
Dominant Taxa	--	Orthocladiinae	Orthocladiinae
Hilsenhoff Biotic Index*	0	5.88	5.48
# of Intolerant Taxa*	0	0	0
# of Tolerant Taxa*	0	1	0
USFS Community Tolerance Quotient (d)*	0	103	108
# of shredder taxa*	0	1	0
# of scraper taxa*	0	0	0
# of collector-filterer taxa*	0	0	0
# of collector-gatherer taxa*	0	4	4
# of predator taxa*	0	2	1
# of clinger taxa*	0	0	0
Long-lived Taxa*	0	2	1

Coliform

Status:

The coliform sample from Jim Ford Creek indicates that in late August *E. coli* levels (33.5 MPN/100 ml) fell below the state standard for individual samples (< 406 *E. coli*/100 ml) (Table 8). Fecal coliform (33.0 MPN/100ml) was also well below the state standard of <500/100 ml. Note that *E. coli* is now used as the primary indicator for human pathogens rather than fecal coliform.

Table 8. Results of coliform samples taken in the Jim Ford Creek in August 2011.

Sample Date	Location	Total Coliform	Fecal Coliform	E. coli
8/24/2011	Jim Ford Creek– approx. 150 m downstream of the bridge.	>2419.2 MPN/100 ml	33.0 /100 ml	33.5 MPN/100 ml

MPN= most probable number

Lapwai Creek- Spalding

Water Chemistry:

Cross Section Survey:
A cross section survey was conducted at the proposed multiprobe deployment location to evaluate if the site was reasonably representative of stream conditions throughout the park. As suggested by the water resource division the UCBN judges overall representativeness primarily on the basis of specific conductance (Starkey et al. 2008).

The 2011 deployment location provided adequate water depth throughout the field season, was easily accessible, and was away from heavily trafficked access points.

A one way analysis of variance (ANOVA) test was conducted to evaluate representativeness (R v2.12.0). Results of the ANOVA showed that there was a significant difference for specific conductance among the transects and the deployment location in June $F_{(4,34)}= 27.062$, $p< 0.05$ and a significant difference in September $F_{(4,39)}= 14.64$, $p < 0.05$.

To determine where the difference in representativeness occurred, a post hoc Tukey's test was conducted (R v2.12.0). Relative to specific conductance, results of the Tukey's test for the cross section conducted in June indicates that the deployment location was significantly different from transect 3 and 4 (Figure 13). Results of the Tukey's test for the cross section conducted in September indicates that the deployment location was significantly different from transect 2, 3 and 4 (Figure 14).

It should be noted that transects 3 and 4 occurred at or just upstream of the two bridges within the park. Reasons for the difference between the deployment location and transects 3 and 4 appeared to be related to the influence of these bridges. During the cross section survey, specific conductance was notably different near these structures.

In summary, the deployment location was less representative of upstream conditions than desirable; however, there are currently no other suitable pools within the park for deployment. In addition, the deployment location is likely more representative of conditions downstream (i.e., away from the bridges). In the future, the UCBN may consider a cross section survey in the opposite direction (i.e., downstream of deployment location) to determine if this is a valid assumption.

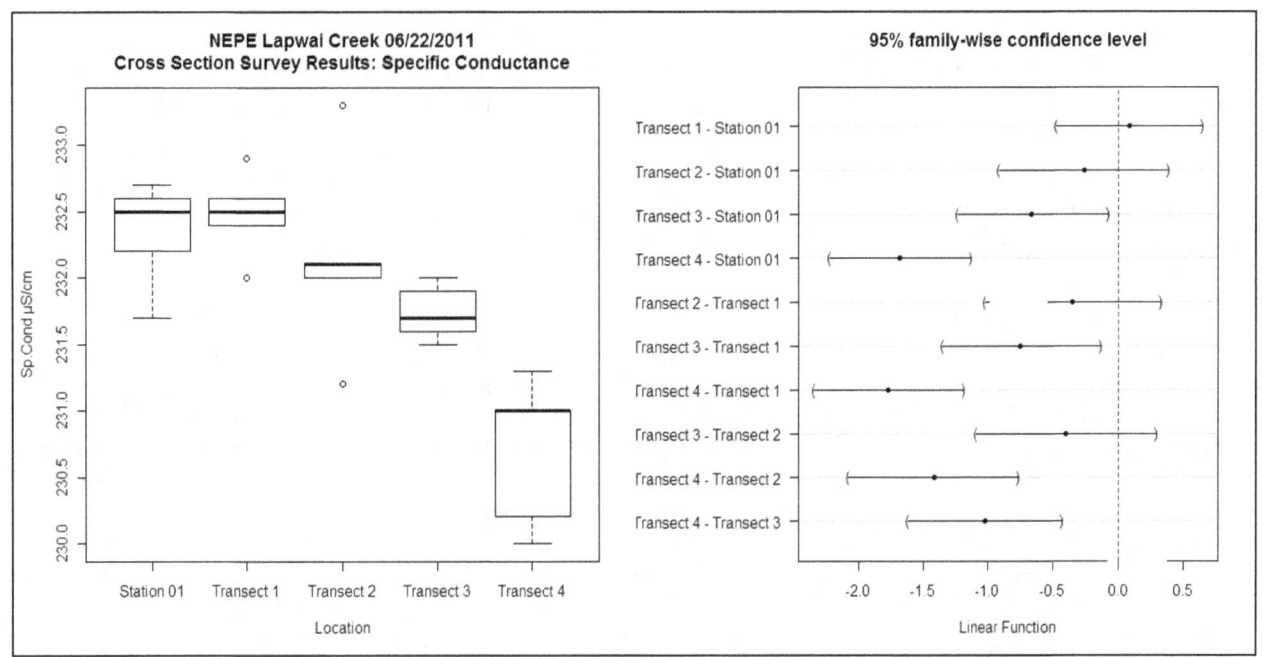

Figure 13. June 2011 cross section survey of Lapwai Creek, box plot of specific conductance and plot of 95% family-wise confidence level.
Note that "Station 01" is the location of multiprobe deployment and the transects progress upstream (1-4).

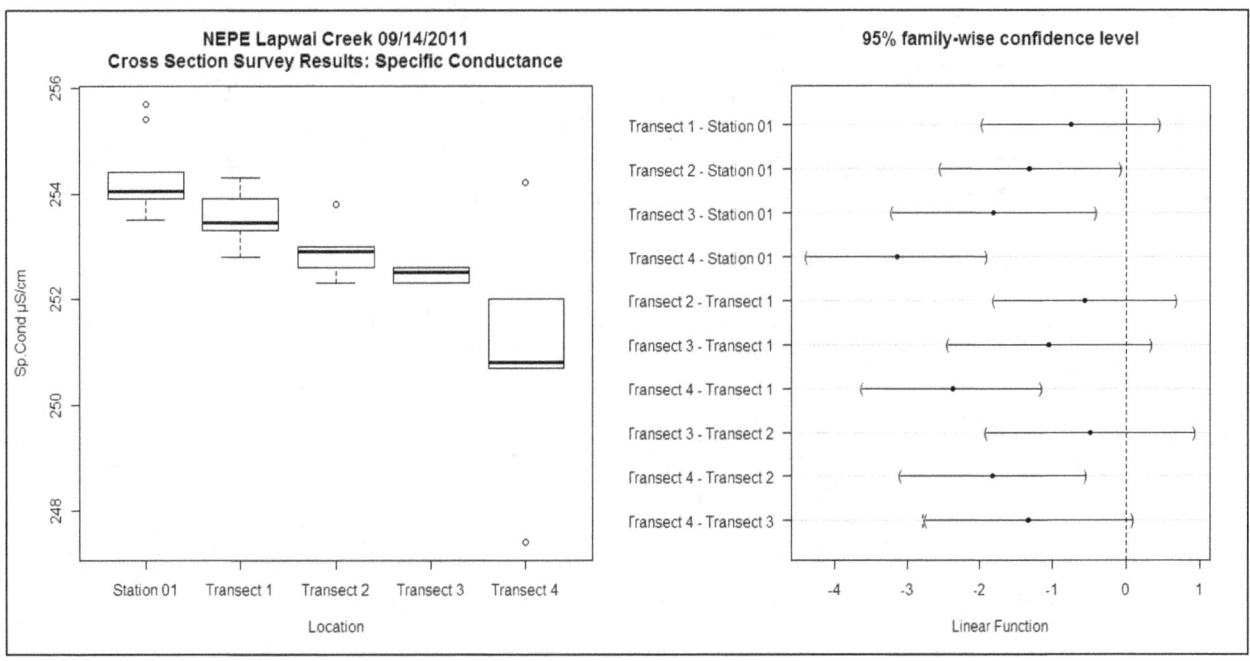

Figure 14. September 2011 cross section survey of Lapwai Creek, box plot of specific conductance and plot of 95% family-wise confidence level.
Note that "Station 01" is the location of multiprobe deployment and the transects progress upstream (1-4).

Status:

Condition of core water quality parameters (2011) along with the corresponding Idaho DEQ regulatory threshold are given in Table 9. For comparison, the condition of core water quality parameters as observed in 2008 are given in Table 10. As in Jim Ford Creek, the primary concern in Lapwai Creek is elevated water temperatures and its effect on native salmonids. In addition, Lapwai Creek regularly exceeded the upper pH criteria which may have a detrimental effect on native aquatic biota.

Table 9. Vital sign summary table for water chemistry in Lapwai Creek June-November, 2011.

Lapwai Creek Water Chemistry Summary 2011

Measure	Current Condition (June-November, 2011)	State DEQ Thresholds [a]	% Exceedance [b]
Temperature (*MDMT, **MDAT)	* MDMT= 24.31 °C ** MDAT= 21.04 °C	*MDMT<22 °C **MDAT<19 °C	27% 17%
Specific conductance (mean)	273.19 µS/cm	N/A	N/A
Dissolved oxygen (mean daily min)	8.24 mg/L	> 6.0 mg/L	0%
pH (mean daily max)	9.0 pH Units	9.0 pH Units, Max	14%
pH (mean daily min)	7.9 pH Units	6.5 pH Units, Min	0%
Turbidity (mean daily max)	104 NTU[c]	< 50 NTU over background (instantaneous) < 25 for 10 consecutive days	Insufficient data
E. coli	46.7 MPN/100 ml	< 406 E. coli/100 ml	0%
Fecal Coliform	22 MPN/100ML	<500 cfu/100 ml	0%

*MDMT – Maximum Daily Maximum Temperature, **MDAT – Maximum Daily Average Temperature, [a]Criteria for cold water life designation, [b] Proportion of samples above water quality standard [c]Mean daily max based on 2 months of data due to poor data quality, see Table 1 for an explanation of color coding.

Table 10. Vital sign summary table for water chemistry in Lapwai Creek June-November, 2008.

Lapwai Creek Water Chemistry Summary 2008

Measure	Current Condition (June-November, 2008)	State DEQ Thresholds [a]	% Exceedance [b]
Temperature (*MDMT, **MDAT)	* MDMT= 27.88 °C ** MDAT= 22.95 °C	*MDMT<22 °C **MDAT<19 °C	38% 31%
Specific conductance (mean)	220.55 µS/cm	N/A	N/A
Dissolved oxygen (mean daily min)	7.58 mg/l	> 6.0 mg/l	2 %
pH (mean daily max)	8.9 pH Units	9.0 pH Units, Max	5%
pH (mean daily min)	7.9 pH Units	6.5 pH Units, Min	0%
Turbidity (mean daily max)	9.6 NTU	< 50 NTU over background (instantaneous) < 25 for 10 consecutive days	Insufficient data

*MDMT – Maximum Daily Maximum Temperature, **MDAT – Maximum Daily Average Temperature , [a]Criteria for cold water life designation [b] Proportion of samples above water quality standard, see Table 1 for an explanation of color coding.

- *Temperature:*
  The maximum daily maximum temperature (MDMT) exceeded 22.0 °C in 27% of observations and the maximum daily average temperature (MDAT) exceeded 19 °C in 17% of observations. In 2011, both MDMT and MDAT exceedances were less than in 2008, 38% and 31% respectively. Despite less frequent exceedance, our data reinforces basin-wide temperature concerns as mentioned in the 1998 303(d) list, Lapwai Creek Aquatic Assessment (Cichosz et al. 2001), and Lapwai Creek Watershed Ecological Restoration Strategy (Richardson et al. 2009). Figure 15 shows the daily maximum and mean daily temperatures in Lapwai Creek from June-November 2011. Table 11 lists the data rating/grade for each deployment period (monthly interval). These standard USGS ratings are based on the degree of sensor fouling and drift encountered during each deployment period (Wagner et al. 2006; Starkey et al. 2008).

  Water temperatures are of particular interest in Lapwai Creek, given that its designated use includes cold water biota and that it provides habitat for the following anadramous fish species: steelhead (*Oncorhynchus mykiss*),.chinook salmon (*Oncorhynchus tshawytscha*), coho salmon (*Oncorhynchus kisutch*), and lamprey (*Lampreta tridentate*) (Richardson et al. 2009). Implications of elevated water temperatures may include decreased salmonid recruitment, decreased salmonid health, and potential shifts in fish and benthic macroinvertebrate communities (Vannote and Sweeney 1980; McCullough 1999). It is also important to note that elevated water temperatures have the capacity to reduce the total concentration of dissolved oxygen (i.e., there is an inverse relationship between water temperature and dissolved oxygen; Figure 17), thereby impacting aquatic biota.

  Maintaining water temperatures suitable for naturally occurring species in Lapwai Creek will depend on riparian and stream channel conditions basin wide. For this reason cooperation with other agencies, stakeholders, and adjacent landowners will be critical for improving water temperature.

- *Specific Conductance:*
  Specific conductance ranged from 200.1 to 300.7 µS/cm, with an average specific conductance of 273.2 µS/cm (Figure 16). Table 12 shows the data rating/grade for each deployment period (monthly interval). These standard USGS ratings are based on the degree of sensor fouling and drift encountered during each deployment period (Wagner et al. 2006; Starkey et al. 2008). The specific conductance data grade of "poor" was primarily due to sever sensor fouling. Corrections that have been applied to the specific conductance data are listed in Appendix E.

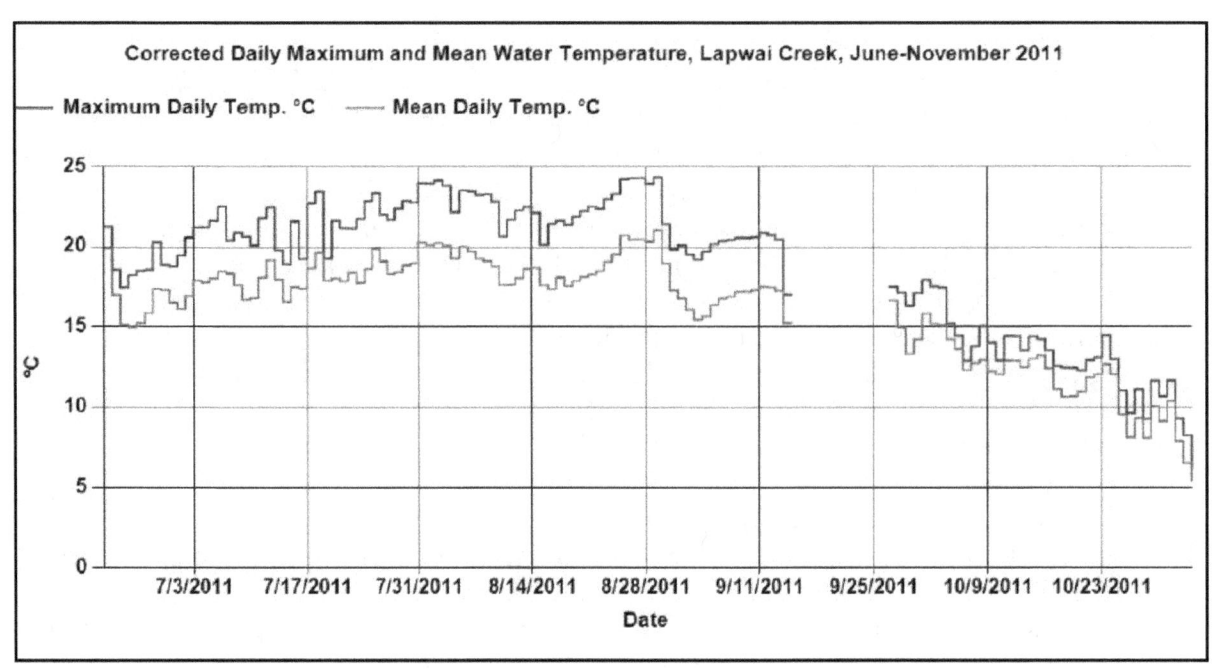

Figure 15. Daily maximum and mean temperature in Lapwai Creek, NEPE, 2011.

Table 11. Data grade/rating for water temperature each deployment period June-November 2011 in Lapwai Creek, NEPE.

Temperature Data Grade/Rating	From UTC-07:00	To UTC-07:00
EXCELLENT	6/22/2011 12:00	7/13/2011 8:00
EXCELLENT	7/13/2011 17:00	8/17/2011 8:00
EXCELLENT	8/17/2011 13:00	9/14/2011 8:00
EXCELLENT	9/27/2011 15:00	11/3/2011 11:00

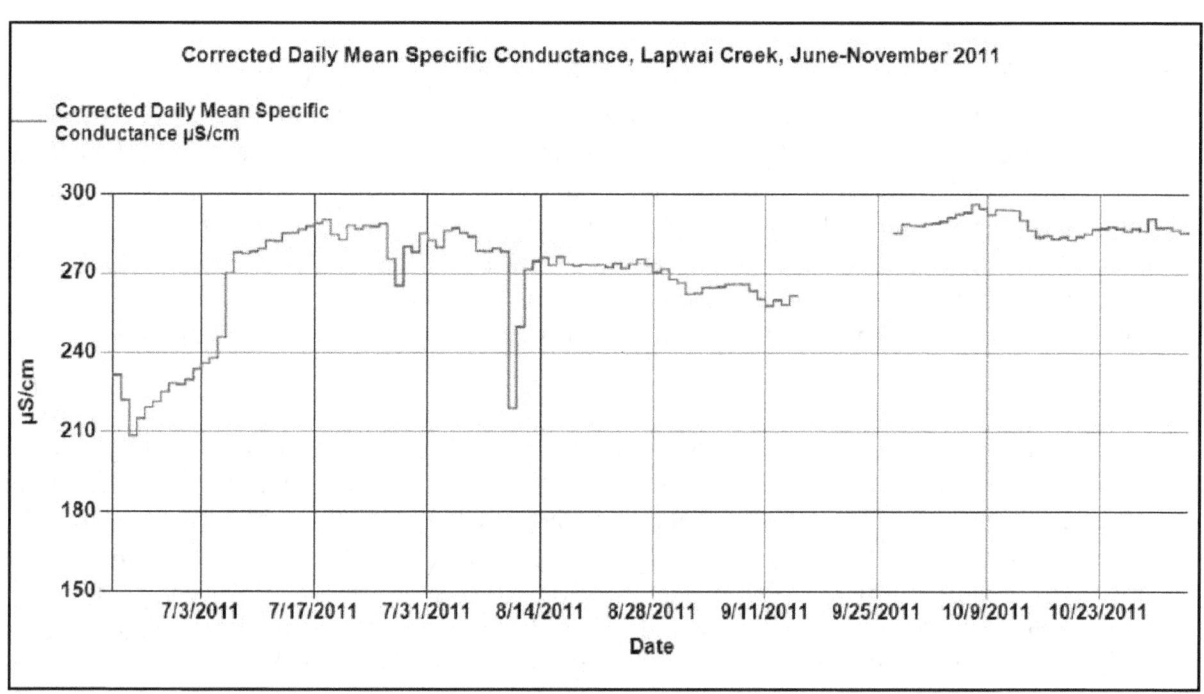

Figure 16. Corrected mean daily specific conductance in Lapwai Creek, NEPE, 2011.

Table 12. Data grade/rating for specific conductance each deployment period June-November 2011 in Lapwai Creek, NEPE.

Specific Conductance Data Grade/Rating	From UTC-07:00	To UTC-07:00
GOOD	6/22/2011 12:00	7/13/2011 8:00
GOOD	7/13/2011 17:00	8/17/2011 8:00
GOOD	8/17/2011 13:00	9/14/2011 8:00
POOR	9/27/2011 15:00	11/3/2011 11:00

31

- *Dissolved Oxygen:*
  Mean daily minimum dissolved oxygen was 8.6 mg/L and was never below the regulatory threshold (6.0 mg/L). In 2008, 2% of observations fell below 6.0 mg/l. Figure 17 shows the daily minimum dissolved oxygen and maximum temperatures in Lapwai Creek from June-November 2011. Table 13 shows the data rating/grade for each deployment period (monthly interval). These standard USGS ratings are based on the degree of sensor fouling and drift encountered during each deployment period (Wagner et al. 2006; Starkey et al. 2008). The data grade of "poor" was due to a combination of calibration drift and sensor fouling. Corrections that have been applied to the dissolved oxygen data are listed in Appendix E.

- *pH:*
  The minimum and maximum pH was 7.25 and 9.67 pH units respectively. pH exceeded the upper threshold of 9.0 pH units in 14% of observations. It should be noted that in 2008, pH exceeded the upper pH criteria (9.0 pH units) in 5% of observations. No observations fell below the lower pH threshold (6.5 pH units). Figure 18 shows the daily maximum, minimum, and median pH in Lapwai Creek from June-November 2011. Table 14 shows the data rating/grade for each deployment period (monthly interval). These standard USGS ratings are based on the degree of sensor fouling and drift encountered during each deployment period (Wagner et al. 2006; Starkey et al. 2008). Data grades less than "excellent" were primarily due to sensor fouling and to a lesser extent sensor drift. Corrections that have been applied to the pH data are listed in Appendix E.

  Elevated pH may be cause for concern as it may indicate pollution from an upstream source. Monitoring of pH in 2014 will help establish if there is an increasing trend for pH levels in Lapwai Creek.

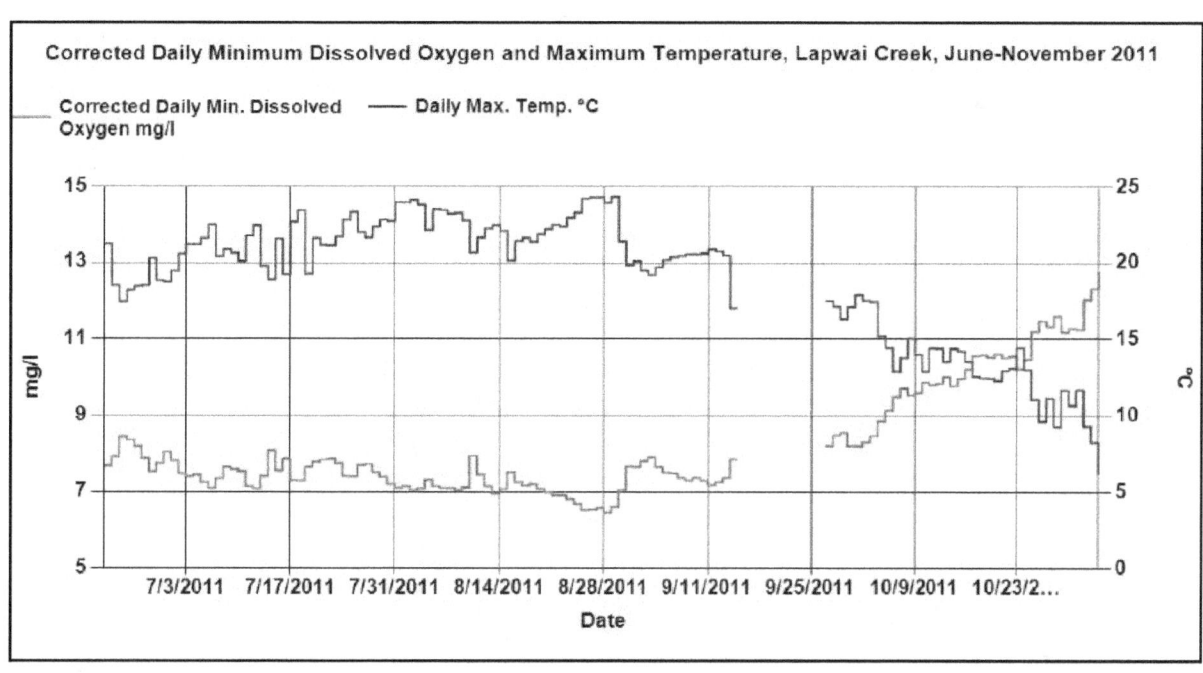

Figure 17. Corrected daily minimum dissolved oxygen and daily maximum temperature in Lapwai Creek, NEPE, 2011.

Table 13. Data grade/rating for dissolved oxygen each deployment period June-November 2011 in Lapwai Creek, NEPE.

Dissolved Oxygen Data Grade/Rating	From UTC-07:00	To UTC-07:00
EXCELLENT	6/22/2011 12:00	7/13/2011 8:00
EXCELLENT	7/13/2011 17:00	8/17/2011 8:00
EXCELLENT	8/17/2011 13:00	9/14/2011 8:00
POOR	9/27/2011 15:00	11/3/2011 11:00

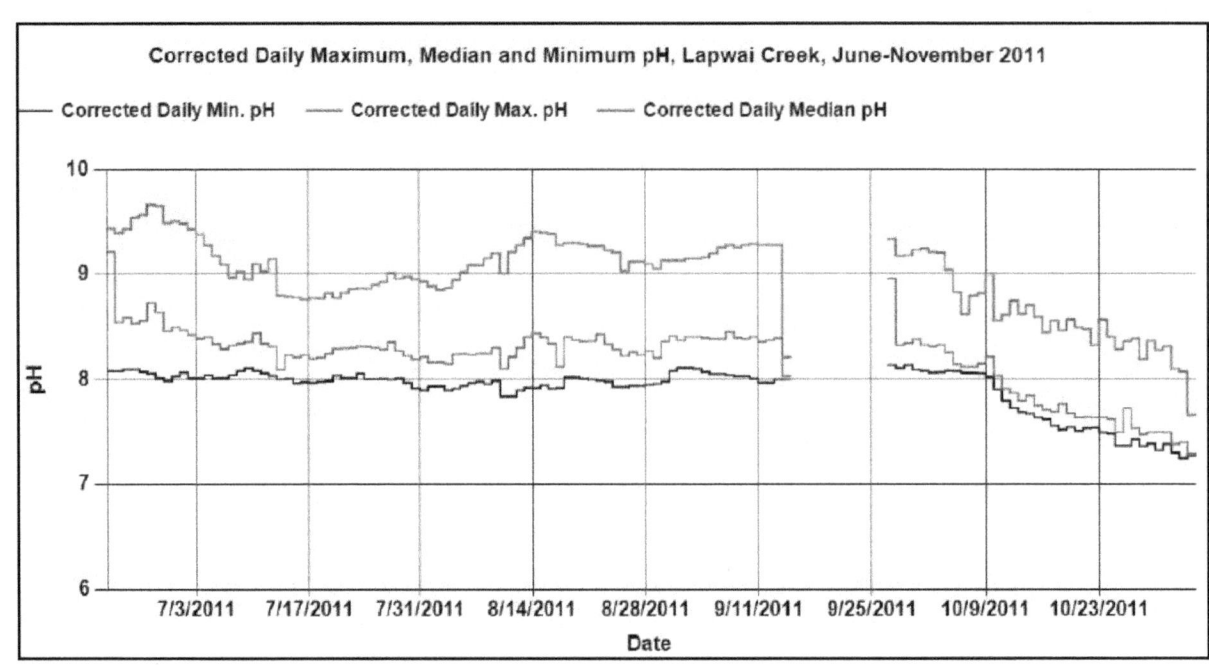

Figure 18. Corrected daily maximum, minimum, and median pH in Lapwai Creek, NEPE, 2011.

Table 14. Data grade/rating for pH each deployment period June-November 2011 in Lapwai Creek, NEPE.

pH Data Grade/Rating	From UTC-07:00	To UTC-07:00
GOOD	6/22/2011 12:00	7/13/2011 8:00
GOOD	7/13/2011 17:00	8/17/2011 8:00
EXCELLENT	8/17/2011 13:00	9/14/2011 8:00
GOOD	9/27/2011 15:00	11/3/2011 11:00

- *Turbidity:*

  Prior to discussion about turbidity in Lapwai Creek, it should be noted that conclusions based on this data are limited due to marginal data quality (Figure 19, Table 15). A combination of sensor fouling and drift influenced data quality. In addition, the turbidity sensor was sent in for repair following the site visit/calibration on September 14th 2011. Sensor failure may have also contributed to the "poor" and "unusable" data grades.

  It is important to note that the method detection limit (MDL) for this sensor was 0.2 NTU and the minimum level of quantitation (ML) was 0.78 NTU (Appendix D). Figure 19 shows the daily mean turbidity in Lapwai Creek from June-November 2011. Corrections that have been applied to turbidity data are listed in Appendix E. Data indicates that turbidity ranged from 1.9 to 1235 NTU. However, due to poor data quality and lack of historic data for this site the UCBN is unable to determine if conditions exceeded state criteria. Regulatory thresholds for turbidity state that it should be "< 50 NTU over background (instantaneous) and < 25 NTU for 10 consecutive days." Although

34

conclusions are limited based on the quality of data collected in 2011 it is likely that Lapwai Creek does experience pulses of turbidity due to upstream agricultural activity and road work.

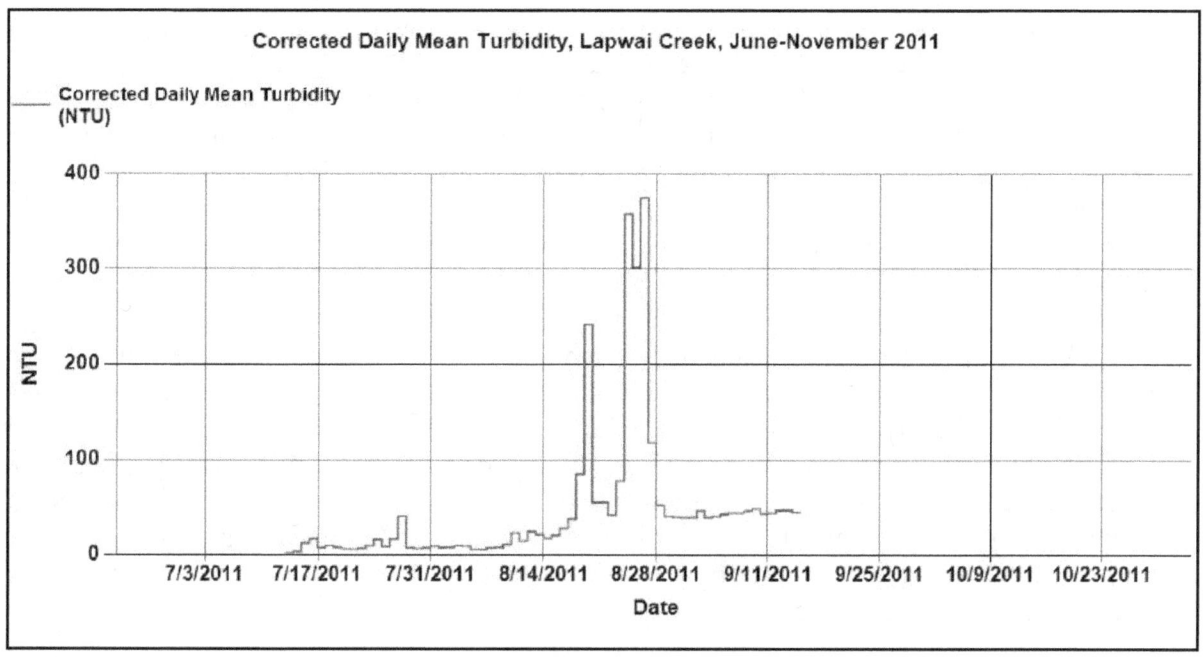

Figure 19. Corrected daily mean turbidity in Lapwai Creek, NEPE, 2011.
Note that the "unusable" (blue) and "poor" (red) data grades presented in table 15 were due to severe fouling and sensor failure.

Table 15. Data grade/rating for turbidity each deployment period June-November 2011 in Lapwai Creek, NEPE.

Turbidity Data Grade/Rating	From UTC-07:00	To UTC-07:00
UNUSABLE	6/22/2011 12:00	7/13/2011 8:00
POOR	7/13/2011 17:00	8/17/2011 8:00
POOR	8/17/2011 13:00	9/14/2011 8:00
UNUSABLE	9/27/2011 15:00	11/3/2011 11:00

Macroinvertebrates

Status:

The Hilsenhoff Biotic Index (HBI), which summarizes pollution tolerances of the macroinvertebrate taxa within the sample, indicates that Lapwai Creek has "fairly substantial [organic] pollution likely" and "fair" water quality (HBI= 5.17) (Hilsenhoff 1987, 1988). HBI values generally increase (HBI ranges from 0.0 to 10.0) as nutrient enrichment increases. While HBI is most sensitive to organic pollution, it may also respond to sediment loading, low dissolved oxygen and elevated water temperatures. The US Forest Service (USFS) community tolerance quotient was 91 and indicates that Lapwai Creek is impaired. Values of the USFS tolerance quotient range from 20 to just over 100, with lower values indicating better water quality.

The number of Ephemeroptera, Plecoptera, Trichoptera (EPT) taxa was 7; there were 2 long lived taxa; and the dominate family was Simuliidae (black flies). These data along with the tolerance indices listed above suggest that, while Lapwai Creek is in better condition than Jim Ford Creek, it is still impaired. Causes of impairment may be tied to elevated water temperatures, and pH. At the time this report was written, stream channel data from the UCBN's stream channel characteristics monitoring protocol were not available. However, this data may indicate that physical factors (substrate armoring, bank stabilization, bank erosion, etc.) are negatively impacting benthic assemblages.

The observed to expected ratio (OE) for this sample reach was 0.41 and indicated that Lapwai Creek was in "poor" condition. However, due to physiographic and climatic conditions at the sample location the model had to extrapolate rather than interpolate predictor variables. As a result the condition rating should be interpreted with caution. See Table 23 and Appendix F for additional summary metrics.

Table 16. Vital sign summary table for benthic macroinvertebrates in Lapwai Creek, 2011. Note that the entire macroinvertebrate taxa and metrics lists can be found in Appendix F and G.

Lapwai Creek Macroinvertebrate Summary August 2011	
PIBO Station	**3114**
Sample ID	**147157**
Richness*	15
Shannon's Diversity*	1.79
Simpson's Diversity*	0.77
Evenness*	0.66
# of EPT Taxa*	7
Dominant Family	Simuliidae
Dominant Taxa	Simulium
Hilsenhoff Biotic Index*	5.17
# of Intolerant Taxa*	1
# of Tolerant Taxa*	0
USFS Community Tolerance Quotient (d)*	91
# of shredder taxa*	1
# of scraper taxa*	2
# of collector-filterer taxa*	2
# of collector-gatherer taxa*	5
# of predator taxa*	1
# of clinger taxa*	6
Long-lived Taxa*	2

Coliform

Status:

The coliform sample from Lapwai Creek indicates that in late August *E. coli* levels (46.7 MPN/100 ml) fell below the state standard for individual samples (< 406 *E. coli*/100 ml) (Table 17). Fecal coliform (22.0 MPN/100ml) was also well below the state standard of <500/100 ml. Note that *E. coli* is now used as the primary indicator for human pathogens rather than fecal coliform.

Table 17. Results of coliform samples taken in the Lapwai Creek in August 2011.

Sample Date	Location	Total Coliform	Fecal Coliform	*E. coli*
8/24/2011	Lapwai Creek– approx. 100 m downstream of the railroad bridge.	>1986.3 MPN/100 ml	22.0 /100 ml	46.7 MPN/100 ml

MPN= most probable number

Literature Cited

Barbour, M. T., J. Gerritsen, B. D. Snyder, and J. B. Stribling. 1999. Rapid Bioassessment Protocols for Use in Streams and Wadeable Rivers: Periphyton, Benthic Macroinvertebrates and Fish, Second Edition. EPA 841-B-99-002. U.S. Environmental Protection Agency.

Cichosz, T., A. Davidson, C. Rabe, and D. Saul. 2001. Lapwai Creek aquatic assessment. Center for Environmental Education. Washington State University. Pullman, WA. (http://nezperceswcd.org/Portals/2/DocumentLibrary/Publications/Lapwai_Aquatic_Asse ssment.pdf). Accessed 15 December 2011.

Clark, K. 2005. Jim Ford Creek water quality monitoring report 2003-2004. Technical Results Summary KPC-JF-05. Idaho Association of Soil Conservation Districts. Moscow, ID.

Erixson J. A., J. Bell, and D. Hinson. 2010. Natural resource condition assessment: Nez Perce National Historic Park. Natural Resource Technical Report NPS/UCBN/NRTR— 2010/333. National Park Service, Fort Collins, CO.

Garrett, L. K., T. J. Rodhouse, G. H. Dicus, C. C. Caudill, and M. R. Shardlow. 2007. Vitals Signs Monitoring Plan, Upper Columbia Basin Network. Natural Resource Report NPS/PWR/UCBN/NRR—2007/002. National Park Service, Fort Collins, CO.

Heitke, J. D., E. J. Archer, D. D. Dugaw, B. A. Bouwes, E. A. Archer, R. C. Henderson, J. L. Kershner. 2008. Effectiveness monitoring for streams and riparian areas: sampling protocol for stream channel attributes. PACFISH/INFISH- Biological Opinion Effectiveness Monitoroing Program (PIBO-EM). Logan, UT. (http://www.fs.fed.us/biology/fishecology/emp). Accessed 18 January 2010.

Hilsenhoff, W. L. 1987. An improved biotic index of organic stream pollution. Great Lakes Entomologist **20:**31-39.

Idaho Administrative Code. 2011. Idaho administrative code-Department of Environmental Quality, IDAPA 58.01.02 water quality standards. Idaho Department of Environmental Quality, Boise, ID. (http://adm.idaho.gov/adminrules/rules/idapa58/58index.htm). Accessed 14 December 2011.

Idaho Department of Environmental Quality (ID DEQ). 2011. Idaho Department of Environmental Quality Final 2010 Integrated Report. ID DEQ. Boise, ID.

Idaho Department of Environmental Quality (ID DEQ), and Nez Perce Tribe Environmental Protection Agency (EPA). 2000. Jim Ford Creek Total Maximum Daily Load Watershed Management Plan. (http://www.deq.idaho.gov/media/454495- water_data_reports_surface_water_tmdls_jim_ford_creek_jim_ford_entire.pdf). Accessed 9 December 2011.

Irwin, R. J. 2008. Draft Part B lite QA/QC review checklist for aquatic vital sign monitoring protocols and SOPs, National Park Service, Water Resources Division. Fort Collins, CO. (http://www.nature.nps.gov/water/Vital_Signs_Guidance/Guidance_Documents/PartBLite.pdf). Accessed 18 February 2010.

McCullough, D. A. 1999. A review and synthesis of effects of alterations to the water temperature regime on freshwater life stages of salmonids, with special reference to chinook salmon. EPA 910-R-99-010. U.S. Environmental Protection Agency, Washington, DC.

National Park Service (NPS) 1997. Baseline water quality data inventory and analysis: Nez Perce National Historical Park. NPS/NRWRD/NRTR-97/114. Fort Collins, CO.

National Park Service (NPS). 1999. Natural resource challenge: the National Park Service's action plan for preserving natural resources. US Department of the Interior National Park Service, Washington D.C.

National Park Service (NPS). 2000. Strategic plan FY 2001-2005. NPS D-1383. US Department of the Interior National Park Service, Washington D.C. (http://planning.nps.gov/document/NPS_strategic_plan.pdf). Accessed 3 March 2011.

Richardson, S., L. Rasmussen, and C. Chandler. 2009. Lapwai Creek watershed ecological restoration strategy. Nez Perce Tribe and Nez Perce Soil and Water Conservation District, Lapwai, ID. (http://nezperceswcd.org/Portals/2/DocumentLibrary/Publications/StrategyfortheRestorationofLapwaiCreekWatershed6_2_09%20RevisionsJune09.pdf). Accessed 15 December 2011.

Starkey, E. N. 2009. Upper Columbia Basin Network integrated water quality annual report 2008: Nez Perce National Historical Park (NEPE) and Whitman Mission National istoric Site (WHMI). Natural Resource Technical Report NPS/UCBN/NRTR—2009/214. National Park Service, Fort Collins, CO. (http://science.nature.nps.gov/im/units/ucbn/reports/index.cfm#IWQ_Mon). Accessed 4 January 2012.

Starkey, E. N., L. K. Garrett, T. J. Rodhouse, G. H. Dicus, and R. K. Steinhorst. 2008. Upper Columbia Basin Network integrated water quality monitoring protocol: Narrative version 1.0. Natural Resource Report NPS/UCBN/NRR—2008/026. National Park Service, Fort Collins, CO. (http://science.nature.nps.gov/im/units/ucbn/reports/index.cfm#IWQ_Mon). Accessed 4 January 2012.

United States EPA. 2001. Environmental Monitoring and Assessment Program (EMAP): National Coastal Assessment Quality Assurance Project Plan 2001-2004. United States Environmental Protection Agency, Office of Research and Development, National Health and Environmental Effects Research Laboratory, Gulf Ecology Division, Gulf Breeze, FL.EPA/620/R-01/002.

United States EPA. 1995. Environmental Monitoring and Assessment Program (EMAP): Laboratory Methods Manual-Estuaries, Volume 1: Biological and Physical Analyses. U.S. Environmental Protection Agency, Office of Research and Development , Narragansett, RI. EPA/620/R-95/008.

Vannote, R. L., and B. W. Sweeney. 1980. Geographic analysis of thermal equilibria: a conceptual model for evaluating the effect of natural and modified thermal regimes on aquatic insect communities. The American Naturalist **115:** 667–695.

Wagner, R. J., R. W. Boulger Jr., C. J. Oblinger, and B. A. Smith. 2006. Guidelines and Standard procedures for continuous water-quality monitors: station operation, record computation, and data reporting: U.S. Geological Survey Techniques and Methods 1–D3, 51.

Appendix A. 2011 Water Quality Monitoring Locations

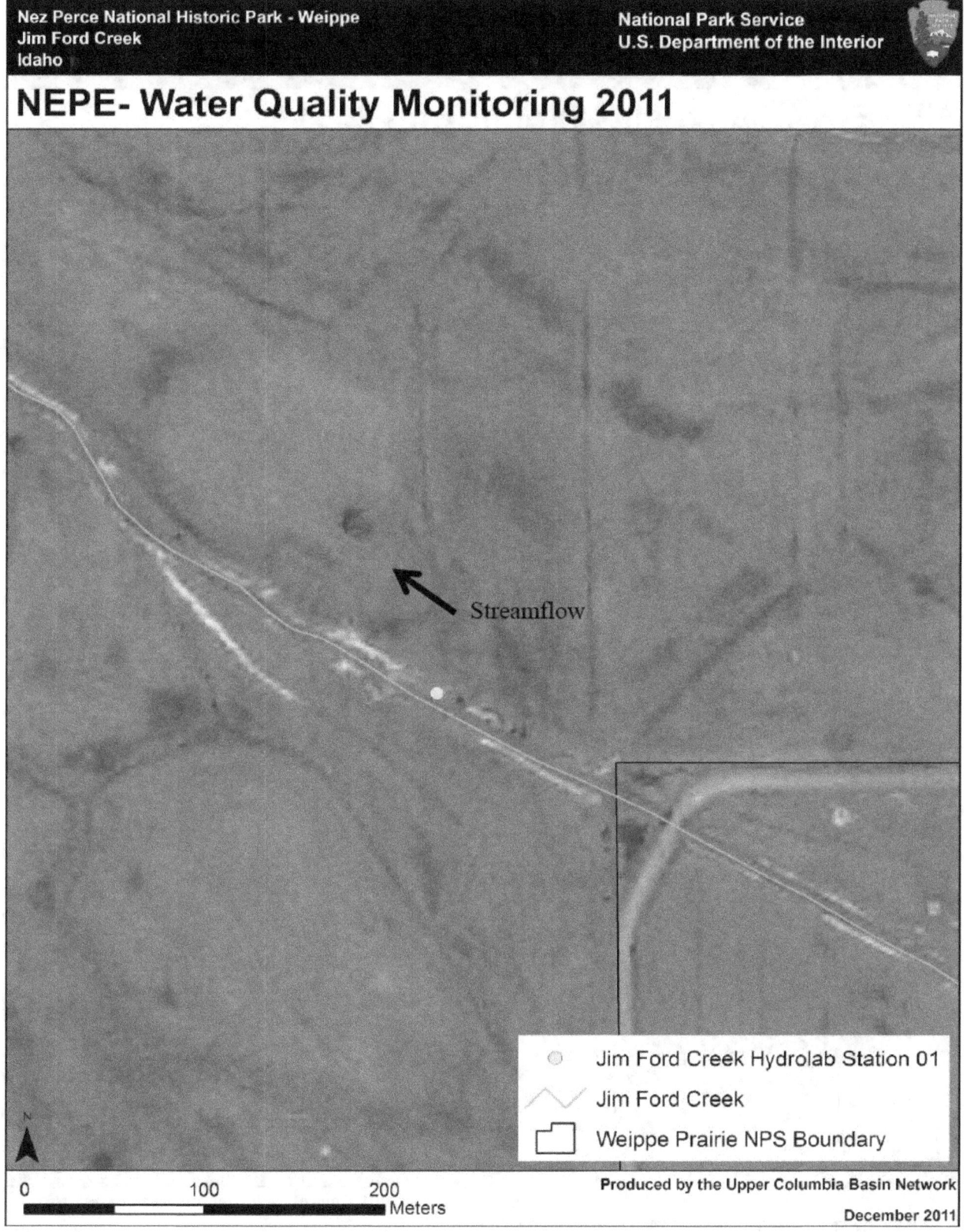

Nez Perce National Historic Park - Weippe
Jim Ford Creek
Idaho

National Park Service
U.S. Department of the Interior

NEPE- Water Quality Monitoring 2011

Streamflow

⊙ Jim Ford Creek Hydrolab Station 01

⋀⋁ Jim Ford Creek

▢ Weippe Prairie NPS Boundary

N

| 0 | 100 | 200 |
Meters

Produced by the Upper Columbia Basin Network

December 2011

Appendix A. 2011 Water Quality Monitoring Locations (continued)

Nez Perce National Historic Park - Spalding
Lapwai Creek
Idaho

National Park Service
U.S. Department of the Interior

NEPE- Water Quality Monitoring 2011

Streamflow

N

○ Lapwai Creek Hydrolab Station 01

〈〉 Lapwai Creek

⬜ Spalding NPS Boundary

0   100   200
                           Meters

Produced by the Upper Columbia Basin Network

December 2011

Appendix B. NEPE Hydrologic Unit Code Boundaries

Nez Perce National Historical Park - Weippe Prairie
Idaho

National Park Service
U.S. Department of the Interior

Hydrologic Unit Code Boundaries

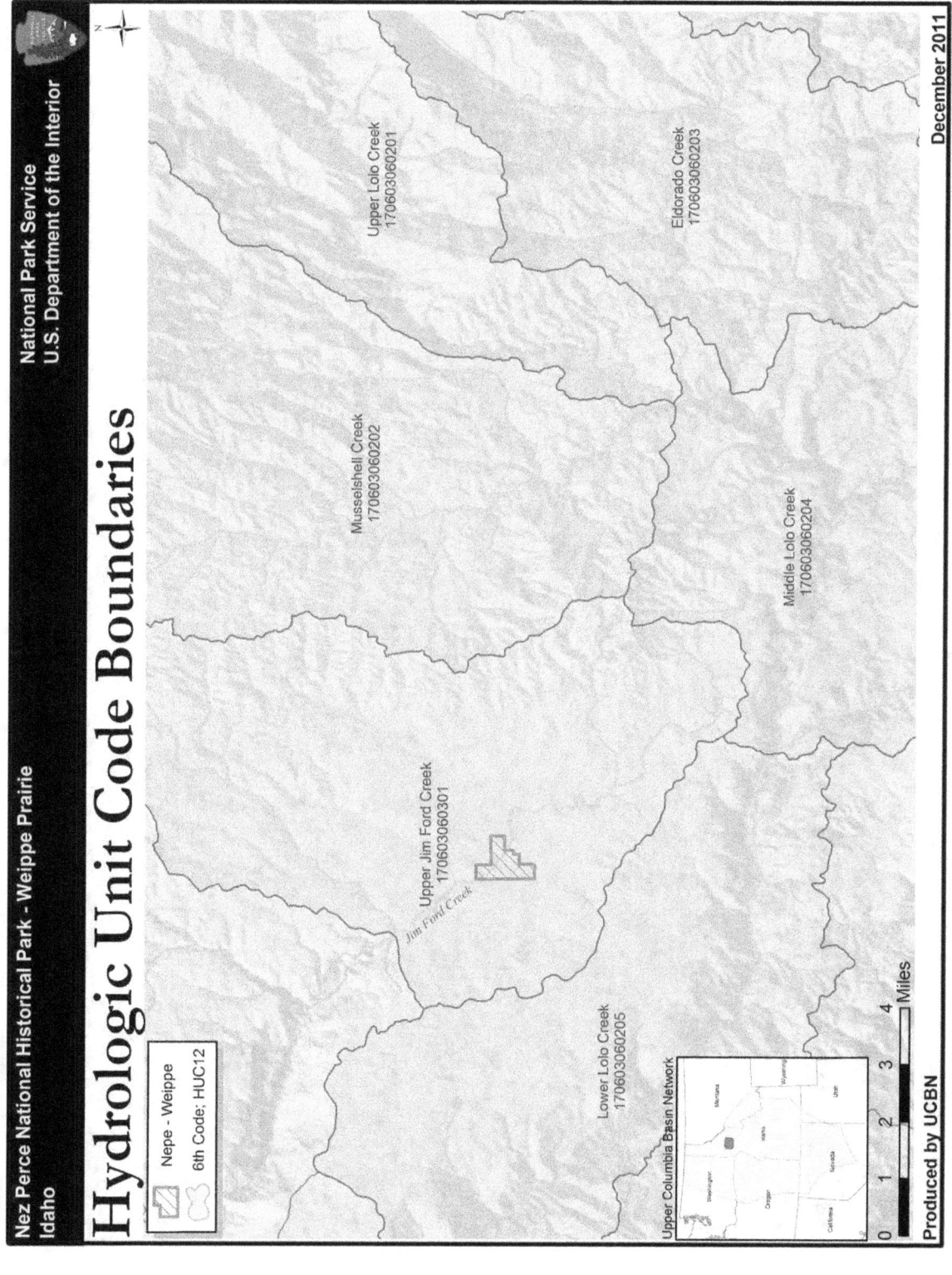

Produced by UCBN

December 2011

45

Appendix B. NEPE Hydrologic Unit Code Boundaries (continued)

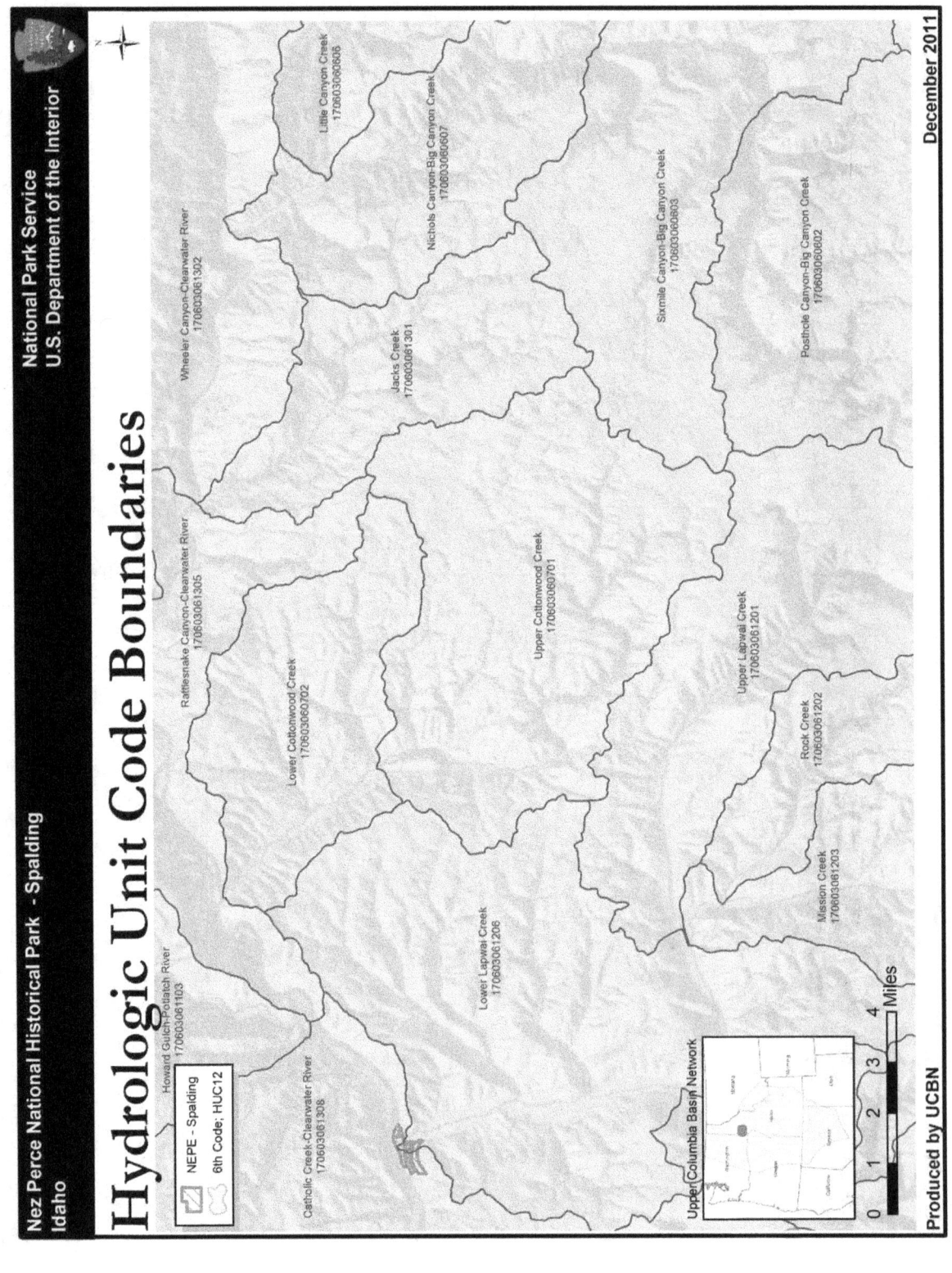

Appendix C. Sample Locations for Water Quality Monitoring at NEPE

Park	Stream	Monitoring Type	Station #	Lat.	Long.	Y	X
NEPE	Jim Ford Creek	Water Chemistry	001	46.35429603	-115.91867957	5133980.86	583193.94
NEPE	Lapwai Creek	Water Chemistry	001	46.44935628	-116.81816423	5143991.41	513966.60
NEPE	Jim Ford Creek	Macroinvertebrates	3115	46.36122	-115.927	5134742	582542
NEPE	Jim Ford Creek	Macroinvertebrates	3116	46.35969	-115.925	5134574	582698
NEPE	Jim Ford Creek	Macroinvertebrates	3118	46.35689	-115.922	5134266	582934
NEPE	Lapwai Creek	Macroinvertebrates	3114	46.45052	-116.818	5144121	513978

Note that X and Y have been projected in WGS84, UTM Zone 11. These locations were recorded by the field crew with a handheld GPS unit.

Appendix D. Quality Control (QC) Indicators

QC data quality indicators for 2011 season at NEPE- Weippe, Jim Ford Creek, Hydrolab #064, Station ID: NEPE-Weippe #001.

STORET Name	Units	Detection Range Description from Manufacture	Method Detection Limit (MDL)	Minimum Level of Quantitation (ML)	Alternative Measurement Sensitivity Plus (AMS+) Beginning of Season	Alternative Measurement Sensitivity Plus (AMS+) End of Season	Precision+ (RPD) Beginning of Season	Precision+ (RPD) End of Season
Temperature, water	deg C	-5 to 50°C	N/A	N/A	0.05	0.02	0.05	0.06
Specific Conductance	µS/cm	0 to 100,000 µS/cm	N/A	N/A	9.7	1.4	2.74	0.69
Dissolved Oxygen	mg/L	0-20 mg/L	N/A	N/A	0.04	0.04	0.25	0.32
pH	pH units	0-14 Units	N/A	N/A	0.03	0.05	0.14	0.14
Turbidity	NTU	0-3000 NTU	0.2	0.53	2.0	3.1	3.13	4.88

QC data quality indicators for 2011 season at NEPE-Spalding, Lapwai Creek Hydrolab #054, Station ID: NEPE-Spalding #001.

STORET Name	Units	Detection Range Description from Manufacture	Method Detection Limit (MDL)	Minimum Level of Quantitation (ML)	Alternative Measurement Sensitivity Plus (AMS+) Beginning of Season	Alternative Measurement Sensitivity Plus (AMS+) End of Season	Precision+ (RPD) Beginning of Season	Precision+ (RPD) End of Season
Temperature, water	deg C	-5 to 50°C	N/A	N/A	0.05	0.12	0.07	0.11
Specific Conductance	µS/cm	0 to 100,000 µS/cm	N/A	N/A	1.3	2.6	0.13	0.12
Dissolved Oxygen	mg/L	0-20 mg/L	N/A	N/A	0.07	0.09	0.00	0.32
pH	pH units	0-14 Units	N/A	N/A	0.14	0.32	0.12	0.81
Turbidity	NTU	0-3000 NTU	0.2	0.78	0.8	N/A	0.00	N/A

Appendix E. Corrections History

Correction history for Jim Ford Creek, NEPE 2011 temperature data.

Creator	Comment	From Time	To Time	Applied Time	Points Modified
N/A	No Corrections Applied	N/A	N/A	N/A	0

Correction history for Jim Ford Creek, NEPE 2011 specific conductance data.

Creator	Comment	From Time	To Time	Applied Time	Points Modified
EStarkey	Drift Correction with Calibration Drift value of 8.50µS/cm and Fouling Drift value of 12.70µS/cm	7/14/2011 17:00	8/18/2011 9:00	8/19/2011 13:56	833
EStarkey	Drift Correction with Calibration Drift value of 0.95µS/cm and Fouling Drift value of 10.00µS/cm	9/1/2011 13:00	10/5/2011 9:00	10/6/2011 14:10	813

Correction history for Jim Ford Creek, NEPE 2011 dissolved oxygen data.

Creator	Comment	From Time	To Time	Applied Time	Points Modified
EStarkey	Drift Correction with Calibration Drift value of -0.08mg/l and Fouling Drift value of 1.24mg/l	6/17/2011 14:00	7/14/2011 9:00	7/18/2011 9:45	644
EStarkey	Delete Region- Sensor Failure	8/7/2011 19:00	8/18/2011 9:00	8/19/2011 14:08	255
EStarkey	Delete Region-Outlier	8/6/2011 22:00	8/7/2011 0:00	8/19/2011 14:09	3
EStarkey	Drift Correction with Calibration Drift value of 8.15mg/l and Fouling Drift value of -0.04mg/l	7/14/2011 17:00	8/18/2011 9:00	8/19/2011 14:19	575

Correction history for Jim Ford Creek, NEPE 2011 pH data.

Creator	Comment	From Time	To Time	Applied Time	Points Modified
EStarkey	Drift Correction with Calibration Drift value of 0.09pH Units and Fouling Drift value of 0.24pH Units	6/17/2011 14:00	7/14/2011 9:00	7/18/2011 9:47	644
EStarkey	Drift Correction with Calibration Drift value of 0.14pH Units and Fouling Drift value of 0.17pH Units	7/14/2011 17:00	8/18/2011 9:00	8/19/2011 14:27	833
EStarkey	Drift Correction with Calibration Drift value of 0.07pH Units and Fouling Drift value of 0.16pH Units	9/1/2011 13:00	10/5/2011 9:00	10/6/2011 14:20	813

Appendix E. Corrections History (continued)

Correction history for Jim Ford Creek, NEPE 2011 turbidity data.

Creator	Comment	From Time	To Time	Applied Time	Points Modified
EStarkey	Drift Correction with Calibration Drift value of -2.35NTU and Fouling Drift value of 5.70NTU	6/17/2011 14:00	7/14/2011 9:00	7/18/2011 9:50	644
EStarkey	Delete point(s) due to outlier	7/1/2011 18:00	7/1/2011 18:00	7/18/2011 9:51	1
EStarkey	Delete point(s) due to outlier	7/7/2011 20:00	7/7/2011 20:00	7/18/2011 9:52	1
EStarkey	Delete point(s) due to outlier	7/8/2011 4:00	7/8/2011 4:00	7/18/2011 9:52	1
EStarkey	Delete Region	8/10/2011 2:00	8/10/2011 2:00	8/19/2011 14:31	1
EStarkey	Drift Correction with Calibration Drift value of 17.10NTU and Fouling Drift value of 8.10NTU	9/1/2011 13:00	10/5/2011 9:00	10/6/2011 14:23	813

Correction history for Lapwai Creek, NEPE 2011 temperature data.

Creator	Comment	From Time	To Time	Applied Time	Points Modified
N/A	No Corrections Applied	N/A	N/A	N/A	0

Correction history for Lapwai Creek, NEPE 2011 specific conductance data.

Creator	Comment	From Time	To Time	Applied Time	Points Modified
EStarkey	Drift Correction with Calibration Drift value of -2.85µS/cm and Fouling Drift value of 4.20µS/cm	6/22/2011 12:00	7/13/2011 8:00	7/18/2011 8:32	501
EStarkey	Drift Correction with Calibration Drift value of -3.85µS/cm and Fouling Drift value of 9.10µS/cm	7/13/2011 17:00	8/17/2011 8:00	8/19/2011 9:47	832
EStarkey	Drift Correction with Calibration Drift value of -4.70µS/cm and Fouling Drift value of 1.30µS/cm	8/17/2011 13:00	9/14/2011 8:00	9/15/2011 11:07	668
EStarkey	Delete Region-the shift in data appears to have been influenced by fouling and not other causes (i.e. no increase in discharge).	10/29/2011 5:00	10/29/2011 19:00	11/9/2011 11:32	15
EStarkey	Delete Region- due to outliers	10/31/2011 20:00	10/31/2011 22:00	11/9/2011 11:32	3
EStarkey	Delete Region- due to outlier	11/1/2011 23:00	11/1/2011 23:00	11/9/2011 11:32	1
EStarkey	Delete Region- due to outliers	11/3/2011 7:00	11/3/2011 11:00	11/9/2011 11:33	5

Appendix E. Corrections History (continued)

Correction history for Lapwai Creek, NEPE 2011 specific conductance data (continued).

Creator	Comment	From Time	To Time	Applied Time	Points Modified
EStarkey	Drift Correction with Calibration Drift value of -3.25µS/cm and Fouling Drift value of 0.00µS/cm. Fouling Drift Correction (46.2) was not applied. The measures just prior to instrument service indicate that fouling within the sensor orifice was likely responsible for low readings. These readings do not appear to have been representative of the deployment period.	9/27/2011 15:00	11/3/2011 11:00	11/9/2011 11:38	861

Correction history for Lapwai Creek, NEPE 2011 dissolved oxygen data.

Creator	Comment	From Time	To Time	Applied Time	Points Modified
EStarkey	Delete Region- Outlier	6/29/2011 16:00	6/29/2011 16:00	8/19/2011 9:57	1
EStarkey	Delete Region- Outlier	8/4/2011 12:00	8/4/2011 12:00	8/19/2011 9:52	1
EStarkey	Drift Correction with Calibration Drift value of 1.30mg/l and Fouling Drift value of 0.42mg/l	9/27/2011 15:00	11/3/2011 11:00	11/9/2011 11:42	885

Correction history for Lapwai Creek, NEPE 2011 pH data.

Creator	Comment	From Time	To Time	Applied Time	Points Modified
EStarkey	Drift Correction with Calibration Drift value of -0.06pH Units and Fouling Drift value of 0.21pH Units	6/22/2011 12:00	7/13/2011 8:00	7/18/2011 8:36	501
EStarkey	Drift Correction with Calibration Drift value of 0.10pH Units and Fouling Drift value of 0.13pH Units	7/13/2011 17:00	8/17/2011 8:00	8/19/2011 10:36	832
EStarkey	Drift Correction with Calibration Drift value of 0.09pH Units and Fouling Drift value of -0.29pH Units	9/27/2011 15:00	11/3/2011 11:00	11/9/2011 11:46	885

Appendix E. Corrections History (continued)

Correction history for Lapwai Creek, NEPE 2011 turbidity data.

Creator	Comment	From Time	To Time	Applied Time	Points Modified
EStarkey	Delete point(s) due to outlier	7/12/2011 19:00	7/12/2011 19:00	7/18/2011 8:38	1
EStarkey	Delete point(s) due to outlier	7/8/2011 6:00	7/8/2011 6:00	7/18/2011 8:48	1
EStarkey	Delete point(s) due to outlier	7/8/2011 14:00	7/8/2011 14:00	7/18/2011 8:48	1
EStarkey	Delete Region-Outlier	7/18/2011 10:00	7/18/2011 10:00	8/19/2011 10:41	1
EStarkey	Delete Region-Outlier	7/18/2011 20:00	7/18/2011 20:00	8/19/2011 10:41	1
EStarkey	Delete Region-Outlier	7/19/2011 23:00	7/19/2011 23:00	8/19/2011 10:42	1
EStarkey	Delete Region-Outlier	7/20/2011 10:00	7/20/2011 10:00	8/19/2011 10:42	1
EStarkey	Delete Region-Outlier	7/21/2011 8:00	7/21/2011 8:00	8/19/2011 10:42	1
EStarkey	Delete Region-Outlier	7/21/2011 5:00	7/21/2011 5:00	8/19/2011 10:42	1
EStarkey	Delete Region-Outlier	7/21/2011 23:00	7/21/2011 23:00	8/19/2011 10:43	1
EStarkey	Delete Region-Outlier	7/22/2011 22:00	7/22/2011 22:00	8/19/2011 10:43	1
EStarkey	Delete Region-Outlier	7/23/2011 15:00	7/23/2011 15:00	8/19/2011 10:43	1
EStarkey	Delete Region-Outlier	7/26/2011 23:00	7/26/2011 23:00	8/19/2011 10:45	1
EStarkey	Delete Region-blocked optic	7/27/2011 18:00	7/27/2011 18:00	8/19/2011 10:46	1
EStarkey	Delete Region-blocked optic	7/27/2011 21:00	7/27/2011 21:00	8/19/2011 10:46	1
EStarkey	Delete Region-Outlier	7/29/2011 3:00	7/29/2011 3:00	8/19/2011 10:46	1
EStarkey	Delete Region-Outlier	7/29/2011 14:00	7/29/2011 14:00	8/19/2011 10:47	1
EStarkey	Delete Region-Outliers	7/30/2011 23:00	7/31/2011 0:00	8/19/2011 10:47	2
EStarkey	Delete Region-Outlier	8/3/2011 6:00	8/3/2011 6:00	8/19/2011 10:48	1
EStarkey	Delete Region-Outlier	8/3/2011 23:00	8/3/2011 23:00	8/19/2011 10:48	1
EStarkey	Delete Region- blocked optic	8/5/2011 6:00	8/5/2011 7:00	8/19/2011 10:49	2
EStarkey	Delete Region-Outlier	8/5/2011 10:00	8/5/2011 10:00	8/19/2011 10:49	1
EStarkey	Delete Region- blocked optic	8/6/2011 0:00	8/6/2011 0:00	8/19/2011 10:49	1
EStarkey	Delete Region-Outlier	8/6/2011 3:00	8/6/2011 3:00	8/19/2011 10:50	1
EStarkey	Delete Region-Outlier	8/6/2011 19:00	8/6/2011 19:00	8/19/2011 10:50	1
EStarkey	Delete Region-Outlier	8/7/2011 2:00	8/7/2011 2:00	8/19/2011 10:50	1
EStarkey	Delete Region-Outlier	8/10/2011 15:00	8/10/2011 15:00	8/19/2011 10:51	1
EStarkey	Delete Region- suspected blocked optic	8/10/2011 18:00	8/10/2011 19:00	8/19/2011 10:51	2
EStarkey	Delete Region-Outlier	7/16/2011 18:00	7/16/2011 18:00	8/19/2011 10:55	1
EStarkey	Delete Region-Outlier	7/16/2011 17:00	7/16/2011 17:00	8/19/2011 10:55	1
EStarkey	Delete Region-Outlier	7/16/2011 15:00	7/16/2011 15:00	8/19/2011 10:56	1
EStarkey	Delete Region-Outlier	7/17/2011 7:00	7/17/2011 7:00	8/19/2011 10:56	1
EStarkey	Delete Region-Outlier	7/17/2011 9:00	7/17/2011 9:00	8/19/2011 10:56	1

Appendix E. Corrections History (continued)

Correction history for Lapwai Creek, NEPE 2011 turbidity data (continued).

Creator	Comment	From Time	To Time	Applied Time	Points Modified
EStarkey	Drift Correction with Calibration Drift value of -0.20NTU and Fouling Drift value of -1.30NTU	7/13/2011 17:00	8/17/2011 8:00	8/19/2011 11:00	799
EStarkey	Delete point(s)	8/23/2011 17:00	8/23/2011 17:00	9/15/2011 11:25	1
EStarkey	Delete Region	8/23/2011 15:00	8/23/2011 16:00	9/15/2011 11:25	2
EStarkey	Revert to Raw data	8/23/2011 17:00	8/23/2011 17:00	9/15/2011 11:25	1
EStarkey	Delete point(s)	8/23/2011 17:00	8/23/2011 17:00	9/15/2011 11:25	1
EStarkey	Revert to Raw data	8/23/2011 15:00	8/23/2011 15:00	9/15/2011 11:25	1
EStarkey	Delete Region- due to outlier	8/26/2011 4:00	8/26/2011 4:00	9/15/2011 11:26	1
EStarkey	Delete point(s)	8/27/2011 17:00	8/27/2011 17:00	9/15/2011 11:27	1
EStarkey	Delete point(s)- due to outlier	8/28/2011 2:00	8/28/2011 2:00	9/15/2011 11:27	1
EStarkey	Delete point(s)- due to outlier	8/28/2011 9:00	8/28/2011 9:00	9/15/2011 11:28	1
EStarkey	Delete point(s)- due to outlier	8/31/2011 2:00	8/31/2011 2:00	9/15/2011 11:29	1
EStarkey	Delete point(s)- due to outlier	9/7/2011 13:00	9/7/2011 13:00	9/15/2011 11:32	1
EStarkey	Delete point(s)- due to outlier	9/11/2011 23:00	9/11/2011 23:00	9/15/2011 11:33	1
EStarkey	Delete point(s)- due to outlier	9/12/2011 20:00	9/12/2011 20:00	9/15/2011 11:33	1
EStarkey	Delete point(s)- due to outlier	9/13/2011 0:00	9/13/2011 0:00	9/15/2011 11:33	1
EStarkey	Drift Correction with Calibration Drift value of 8.35NTU and Fouling Drift value of -0.40NTU	9/27/2011 15:00	11/3/2011 11:00	11/9/2011 11:51	885
EStarkey	Delete Region- due to outliers	9/30/2011 4:00	9/30/2011 4:00	11/9/2011 11:52	1
EStarkey	Delete Region- due to outlier	9/30/2011 16:00	9/30/2011 16:00	11/9/2011 11:52	1

Appendix F. Macroinvertebrate Metrics

NPS Upper Columbia Basin Benthos 2011 – NEPE
*Standardized to OTU and fixed count

SampleID	147158	147159	147160	147157
Station (NAMC)	PIBO:3115	PIBO:3116	PIBO:3118	PIBO:3114
Station (Customer)	6368	6369	6371	6367
Waterbody	Jim Ford 1	Jim Ford 2	Jim Ford 4	Lapwai
County	Clearwater	Clearwater	Clearwater	Nez Perce
State	ID	ID	ID	ID
Latitude	46.36121748	46.35968941	46.35689017	46.45051829
Longitude	-115.926842	-115.9251301	-115.9222344	-116.8179127
Collection Date	8/18/2011	8/18/2011	8/19/2011	8/20/2011
Habitat Sampled	Targeted Riffle	Targeted Riffle	Targeted Riffle	Targeted Riffle
Collection Method	Surber Net	Surber Net	Surber Net	Surber Net
Field Notes	NULL	NULL	NULL	NULL
Lab Notes	NULL	NULL	NULL	NULL
Area sampled (m^2)	0.74	0.74	0.74	0.74
Field Split	100	100	100	100
Lab Split	100	100	100	9.38
Split Count	0	30	27	800
Fixed Count	0	28	23	300
Big Rare Count	0	0	0	12
Richness*	0	7	5	15
Abundance	0	41	36	11542
Shannon's Diversity*	0	1.228090808	1.019496713	1.792943137
Simpson's Diversity*	0	0.600529101	0.545454545	0.77212932
Evenness*	0	0.63111383	0.633448923	0.662078988
# of EPT Taxa*	0	2	0	7
EPT Taxa Abundance	0	3	0	2789
Dominant Family	NULL	Chironomidae	Chironomidae	Simuliidae
Abundance of Dominant Family	0	32	30	4312
Dominant Taxa	NULL	Orthocladiinae	Orthocladiinae	Simulium
Abundance of Dominant Taxa	NULL	23	20	2684
Hilsenhoff Biotic Index*	0	5.857142857	5.47826087	5.166666667
# of Intolerant Taxa*	0	0	0	1
Intolerant Taxa abundance	0	0	0	46
# of Tolerant Taxa*	0	1	0	0
Tolerant Taxa abundance	0	1	0	0
USFS Community Tolerance Quotient (d)*	0	103	108	91
# of shredder taxa*	0	1	0	1
Shredder Abundance	0	1	0	14

Appendix F. Macroinvertebrate Metrics (continued)

NPS Upper Columbia Basin Benthos 2011 – NEPE
*Standardized to OTU and fixed count

SampleID	147158	147159	147160	147157
Station (NAMC)	PIBO:3115	PIBO:3116	PIBO:3118	PIBO:3114
Station (Customer)	6368	6369	6371	6367
Waterbody	Jim Ford 1	Jim Ford 2	Jim Ford 4	Lapwai
County	Clearwater	Clearwater	Clearwater	Nez Perce
State	ID	ID	ID	ID
Latitude	46.36121748	46.35968941	46.35689017	46.45051829
Longitude	-115.926842	-115.9251301	-115.9222344	-116.8179127
Collection Date	8/18/2011	8/18/2011	8/19/2011	8/20/2011
Habitat Sampled	Targeted Riffle	Targeted Riffle	Targeted Riffle	Targeted Riffle
Collection Method	Surber Net	Surber Net	Surber Net	Surber Net
# of scraper taxa*	0	0	0	2
Scraper abundance	0	0	0	88
# of collector-filterer taxa*	0	0	0	2
Collector-filterer abundance	0	0	0	5496
# of collector-gatherer taxa*	0	4	4	5
Collector-gatherer abundance	0	36	35	5352
# of predator taxa*	0	2	1	1
Predator abundance	0	3	1	462
# of clinger taxa*	0	0	0	6
Long-lived Taxa*	0	2	1	2
# of Ephemeroptera taxa*	0	2	0	3
Ephemeroptera abundance	0	3	0	1472
# of Plecoptera taxa*	0	0	0	0
Plecoptera abundance	0	0	0	1
# of Trichoptera taxa*	0	0	0	4
Trichoptera abundance	0	0	0	1315
# of Coleoptera taxa*	0	1	0	2
Coleoptera abundance	0	1	0	130
# of Elmidae Taxa*	0	0	0	2
Elmidae abundance	0	0	0	130
# of Megaloptera taxa*	0	0	0	0
Megaloptera abundance	0	0	0	0
# of Diptera taxa*	0	3	3	4
Diptera abundance	0	32	30	8206
# of Chironomidae taxa*	0	3	3	3
Chironomidae abundance	0	32	30	3879
# of Crustacea taxa*	0	0	0	0
Crustacea abundance	0	0	0	0

AppendixF. Macroinvertebrate Metrics (continued)

NPS Upper Columbia Basin Benthos 2011 – NEPE
*Standardized to OTU and fixed count

SampleID	147158	147159	147160	147157
Station (NAMC)	PIBO:3115	PIBO:3116	PIBO:3118	PIBO:3114
Station (Customer)	6368	6369	6371	6367
Waterbody	Jim Ford 1	Jim Ford 2	Jim Ford 4	Lapwai
County	Clearwater	Clearwater	Clearwater	Nez Perce
State	ID	ID	ID	ID
Latitude	46.36121748	46.35968941	46.35689017	46.45051829
Longitude	-115.926842	-115.9251301	-115.9222344	-116.8179127
Collection Date	8/18/2011	8/18/2011	8/19/2011	8/20/2011
Habitat Sampled	Targeted Riffle	Targeted Riffle	Targeted Riffle	Targeted Riffle
Collection Method	Surber Net	Surber Net	Surber Net	Surber Net
# of Oligochaete taxa*	0	0	0	0
Oligochaete abundance	0	0	0	0
# of Mollusca taxa*	0	0	1	0
Mollusca abundance	0	0	1	0
# of Insect taxa*	0	7	3	13
Insect abundance	0	38	30	11138
# of Non-insect taxa*	0	0	2	2
Non-insect abundance	0	3	7	403

Appendix G. Macroinvertebrate Taxa List

NPS Upper Columbia Basin Benthos 2011 – NEPE
Note that all samples were from targeted riffles and sampled using Surber nets.

SAMPLE	STATION	NAME	SAMP DATE	LAB SPLIT	AREA	TSN	CODE	TAXON	Split Count	Big Rare Count	DENSITY (#/m2)
147160	PIBO:3118	Jim Ford 4	8/19/2011	100	0.74	76484	927	Lymnaea	1	0	1
147160	PIBO:3118	Jim Ford 4	8/19/2011	100	0.74	127917	180	Chironomidae	1	0	1
147160	PIBO:3118	Jim Ford 4	8/19/2011	100	0.74	127994	187	Tanypodinae	1	0	1
147160	PIBO:3118	Jim Ford 4	8/19/2011	100	0.74	128457	184	Orthocladiinae	15	0	20
147160	PIBO:3118	Jim Ford 4	8/19/2011	100	0.74	93294	69	Amphipoda	3	0	4
147160	PIBO:3118	Jim Ford 4	8/19/2011	100	0.74	97336	82	Cambaridae	1	0	1
147160	PIBO:3118	Jim Ford 4	8/19/2011	100	0.74	129228	182	Chironominae	5	0	7
147159	PIBO:3116	Jim Ford 2	8/18/2011	100	0.74	102077	374	Coenagrionidae	1	0	1
147159	PIBO:3116	Jim Ford 2	8/18/2011	100	0.74	113166	683	Hydrochus	1	0	1
147159	PIBO:3116	Jim Ford 2	8/18/2011	100	0.74	128457	184	Orthocladiinae	17	0	23
147159	PIBO:3116	Jim Ford 2	8/18/2011	100	0.74	129228	182	Chironominae	6	0	8
147159	PIBO:3116	Jim Ford 2	8/18/2011	100	0.74	93294	69	Amphipoda	2	0	3
147159	PIBO:3116	Jim Ford 2	8/18/2011	100	0.74	100903	251	Callibaetis	1	0	1
147159	PIBO:3116	Jim Ford 2	8/18/2011	100	0.74	101478	261	Caenis	1	0	1
147159	PIBO:3116	Jim Ford 2	8/18/2011	100	0.74	127994	187	Tanypodinae	1	0	1
147157	PIBO:3114	Lapwai	8/20/2011	9.38	0.74	83005	66	Sperchonidae	16	0	231
147157	PIBO:3114	Lapwai	8/20/2011	9.38	0.74	114205	144	Zaitzevia	2	0	29
147157	PIBO:3114	Lapwai	8/20/2011	9.38	0.74	115398	495	Hydropsychidae	15	0	216
147157	PIBO:3114	Lapwai	8/20/2011	9.38	0.74	115408	497	Cheumatopsyche	36	1	520
147157	PIBO:3114	Lapwai	8/20/2011	9.38	0.74	115453	499	Hydropsyche	31	1	448
147157	PIBO:3114	Lapwai	8/20/2011	9.38	0.74	115629	506	Hydroptilidae	1	0	14
147157	PIBO:3114	Lapwai	8/20/2011	9.38	0.74	127994	187	Tanypodinae	4	0	58
147157	PIBO:3114	Lapwai	8/20/2011	9.38	0.74	135830	200	Empididae	1	0	14
147157	PIBO:3114	Lapwai	8/20/2011	9.38	0.74	82769	58	Trombidiformes	11	0	158
147157	PIBO:3114	Lapwai	8/20/2011	9.38	0.74	100626	280	Epeorus	3	0	43

Appendix G. Macroinvertebrate Taxa List (continued)

NPS Upper Columbia Basin Benthos 2011 – NEPE
Note that all samples were from targeted riffles and sampled using Surber nets.

SAMPLE	STATION	NAME	SAMPDATE	LAB SPLIT	AREA	TSN	CODE	TAXON	Split Count	Big Rare Count	DENSITY (#/m2)
147157	PIBO:3114	Lapwai	8/20/2011	9.38	0.74	100800	250	Baetis	25	2	363
147157	PIBO:3114	Lapwai	8/20/2011	9.38	0.74	103102	469	Skwala	0	1	1
147157	PIBO:3114	Lapwai	8/20/2011	9.38	0.74	114093	121	Elmidae	4	0	58
147157	PIBO:3114	Lapwai	8/20/2011	9.38	0.74	114177	135	Optioservus	2	0	29
147157	PIBO:3114	Lapwai	8/20/2011	9.38	0.74	114180	1076	Optioservus quadrimaculatus	1	0	14
147157	PIBO:3114	Lapwai	8/20/2011	9.38	0.74	115095	480	Trichoptera	4	0	58
147157	PIBO:3114	Lapwai	8/20/2011	9.38	0.74	116318	1488	Onocosmoecus unicolor	1	0	14
147157	PIBO:3114	Lapwai	8/20/2011	9.38	0.74	117159	491	Glossosoma	3	1	45
147157	PIBO:3114	Lapwai	8/20/2011	9.38	0.74	117682	350	Petrophila	1	0	14
147157	PIBO:3114	Lapwai	8/20/2011	9.38	0.74	126640	221	Simuliidae	113	0	1628
147157	PIBO:3114	Lapwai	8/20/2011	9.38	0.74	126774	223	Simulium	186	3	2684
147157	PIBO:3114	Lapwai	8/20/2011	9.38	0.74	127917	180	Chironomidae	27	0	389
147157	PIBO:3114	Lapwai	8/20/2011	9.38	0.74	128457	184	Orthocladiinae	177	3	2554
147157	PIBO:3114	Lapwai	8/20/2011	9.38	0.74	129228	182	Chironominae	61	0	879
147157	PIBO:3114	Lapwai	8/20/2011	9.38	0.74	563956	652	Nemata	1	0	14
147157	PIBO:3114	Lapwai	8/20/2011	9.38	0.74	568598	834	Diphetor hageni	6	0	86

NPS 429/113809, April 2012